Distilling Rose

Distilling Rose

A Family Chronicle

Cynthia Lipton

Lip Pubs Trade Paperbacks

ISBN: 978-0-9846339-0-6
Library of Congress Control Number: 2010918607

Printed in the United States of America

For my family—past, present, and future.

The responsibility of a writer is to excavate the experience of the people who produced him.

— James Baldwin

CHAPTER I

EUTHANASIA

———

I felt numb the day we had to put our geriatric German shepherd down.
The tile floor in the vet's office provided no traction for her crumpled
hind legs, which swung behind her like a trailer she couldn't control. Her
brown eyes were bright in spite of the cataract clouds, and she dog-smiled,
with a soft panting. As we moved into the exam room, Dusty kept her
eyes on me and on my husband to be sure neither of us slipped away.
The doctor came in to give Dusty a tranquilizer shot.

"Just to relax her. I'll be back in fifteen minutes to administer
the euthanasia injection." The vet left us alone to spend some time with
Dusty. I sat on the cold floor next to where she was lying and she rested
her head on my folded knee.

"You are a good dog, Dusty." I kept saying praises and petting her
face. As she relaxed, I felt the sting of tears in my sinus. Dusty's head
got heavier and her eyes drooped from the effects of the drug. Her soft
breathing descended into a purring nasal snore.

"I'm going to see what's going on." I got up and headed toward the sliding pocket door and Dusty flinched. I opened the door a crack to check on the status of the doctor. Dusty lifted her head to track my movements, keeping watch the best she could from her sentry post on the floor.

The doctor came back with an assistant and they lifted Dusty's limp body onto the stainless steel table. I laid my face on her face and grasped handfuls of fur at the scruff of her neck. The doctor shaved a tuft of hair from her forearm paw. The exposed skin was white and I could see the contour of the bone and the vein. Then the doctor looped a tourniquet around her leg and he took a fat syringe filled with pink liquid out of his pocket.

"She'll go fast once I administer the dose."

We nodded. I watched the needle pierce her. The veterinarian loosened the tourniquet and droplets of red blood burst into the syringe barrel. It seemed like an eternity as he pushed the pink liquid into her vein. I watched milliliter after milliliter pushed in through the needle, and all this time I clung to handfuls of skin and scruff. As the pink liquid was injected, I was not aware of any difference in the feel of her body or her fur. She was still warm and her eyes were still opened a crack. I could pet the skin of her face and it seemed like she was looking at me through the slits of her eyes.

When the syringe was empty, the doctor withdrew the needle and pressed his stethoscope against her back to listen for a heartbeat.

"She's gone. Stay with her as long as you want." The doctor left the room and slid the pocket door closed.

Dusty looked comfortable, resting, like she was asleep. I hugged her motionless, peaceful body and cried some more. I picked up the tuft of shaved hair, wrapped it in a Kleenex and shoved it in my pocket. I tucked her worn out collar in my bag. I stared for a long time at her still body on the table, still not convinced she wasn't breathing, sleeping, resting.

When it was time to go, I couldn't close the pocket door on her, but left it part way open so she could watch us leave.

Dusty kept so many of my secrets. She accompanied me when I trespassed into places I shouldn't be. She was my cover story, my companion, and my guard.

We adopted her years ago when she was already an old girl. Dusty was the most loyal and attentive dog with her brown soulful shepherd eyes, her polar-bear-shaped nose, and one flop ear. Maybe that ear was crushed and dog-eared in a car door. She carried this old wound with her into this part of her life. Her teeth were worn down to the gums and she shed so much fluff when we brushed her, we could have made the fur into a small puppy.

Dusty came along the night I sneaked into the cemetery. She was my silent accomplice and never told a soul what we did the night we visited the graves of my ancestors in Memory Gardens.

On one side of the cemetery, the skimpy barbwire fence was broken, and this is where Dusty and I entered the cemetery. I brought her along both for security and as an excuse for why I was walking around at night.

I also brought with me three small votive candles and some bloodroot, signifying family connections. And I brought a big black flashlight, the kind you can use to crack someone in the head if necessary. I had reconnoitered the area and had a plan. I would just walk in through the broken barbwire and place a candle on each grave. The three flat headstones are not adjacent to each other because my great-grandmother, Rose Lipton died in 1961, my grandpa Morrie Lipton died in 1968 and my grandmother Mildred Lipton died on February 2, 1993.

First come, first serve.

I waited for the night of the full moon and parked my car in a small lot on Arnold Industrial Way. As I started walking up the sidewalk toward my pre-designated entry location, I noticed one of the industrial buildings had umbrella tables set up in the parking lot. The interior of the building was bright with fluorescent light. I could watch the scene inside, just like I was watching TV. I saw a woman shuffling across the linoleum floor in slippers and figured this place must be some kind of shelter or halfway house.

I kept moving, slipping from the sidewalk down the embankment to get to the dirt swath that borders the side of the cemetery. I shined the flashlight on the ground ahead of me and marched alongside the fence until we got close to the place where my grand folks are buried. The ground was uneven, like it had been roto-tilled that day. I trudged over the dirt-clods with the dog, who seemed to think this was the same as any normal walk, just darker and lumpier.

We walked right through the broken fence, and we were inside. A glaring spotlight illuminated this back corner of the cemetery, like a stage light, bright and cinematic. I squinted into the glare, and then let the dog loose as I set about my business. Dusty stayed close and sniffed around the stones.

I know where my family members are buried. First I found my great grandmother Rose and I squatted in front of her stone. I fished in my pocket for a candle and the package of bloodroot. I placed the candle on Rose Lipton's stone. As I reached for my lighter, the sound of a car and the movement of headlights startled me.

I stood up in fear as my mind raced with excuses, stories and apologies I would give. I was afraid of being caught; I thought I was busted. The car continued toward me. I didn't move from where I stood as I called Dusty in an urgent whisper. She was my reason for being there. I rehearsed apologies in my head as the car lights shone in my eyes.

To my surprise, the car continued around the circle drive and retreated out of view. Guess they didn't see us, or they didn't care. My heartbeat raced from the sudden adrenalin rush, then I breathed a massive, deep sigh of relief and my pulse began to slow down. I spoke to Dusty, telling her how good she was, as I crouched down and petted her, more for my comfort than hers.

I found the moon obscured by a wisp of fog. But now I refocused on my purpose and placed the first small tea light votive on the stone that says: Rose Lipton 1880-1961. I imagined Rose Lipton's face that I knew from old photographs, her black thick eyebrows and her pure white hair. I was given her name, Rose, as my middle name. How I wished I had known her. I squatted next to her and sprinkled some bloodroot chips on her grave, then lit the candle.

I moved seven or eight steps to the stone of Rose's son, Morrie, my most cherished, bald-headed, Jewish doctor grandpa. The stone says: Dr. M. L. Lipton 1905-1968. I sprinkled some bloodroot and lit his candle before proceeding to the grave that says: Mildred Lipton 1911-1993. I knew her the longest and the best. I remembered lap-sitting and book-reading and the way she laughed. I scattered bloodroot and lit her candle, then I stepped off to the side and watched the triangle of candle flame burn.

I'm struck by the different qualities of light I encountered that night: the fluorescent light from the shelter, the shrouded moonlight, the beam from my flashlight on the dirt-clod ground, the glare of the cemetery spotlight, the flash and panic of the car headlights, and the triangular points of candlelight I left flickering on my ancestors' graves.

That visitation took me back to 1993, the year my Grandmother Mildred died. The hum of traffic from Highway 4 fell like static white noise on Memory Gardens Cemetery. I held my son's hand as we walked paths across wide lawns among flowers and pinwheels and gravestones, trying to find where my Grandma was buried. I'd been there only once before. The office was empty on Sundays and locked. I could find no one there to draw a map to my grandmother's grave. The cemetery grounds stretched for acres, with stones and stones and names and names.

The uneven ground rose and dipped from mounds of earth. Poor Jack wobbled and stumbled while I pulled him along. We walked for a while until we found a bench to sit on. Small tears wet my eyelashes as I looked around and apologized for my neglect. I felt sorry for not visiting my grandmother at the nursing home the day I thought of popping in. On that day, I had shrugged off the urge and went about my business, driving by without stopping. I regret that choice to this day. So on March 14, 1993, I sat on the stone bench, holding my squirming little son, feeling both sad and peaceful, while I missed my grandparents.

It was Grandma's birthday, and with her death being so fresh, the sting hit me even stronger. She'd died six weeks earlier, on February 2, 1993. As I sat there in the middle of my thirtieth year, with my baby son starting his second year, my mind tumbled with thoughts, regrets and remembrance. I carried Jack back to the car and buckled him in. He was glad for the outing and smiled and babbled as we drove off.

At that time I had in my possession two cardboard boxes that contained family papers and sentimental objects. I'd been waiting to look through them for a time when the house was quiet and I was alone. I turned on the desk lamp to light just the corner where I was working. I spread the papers out on the desktop in that dark room and began to read in the circle of the lamp glow. The rest of the room was dark.

In the first box, I found my grandfather's wallet and held the wallet to my nose. The smell of old leather reminded me of how he used to smell when he held me on his lap. He carried this hunk of leather and treasure close to his body, protected from intruders and thieves, for years and years. Now I held that wallet in my hands.

I removed a stack of cards from the first compartment of the wallet. On top was my grandfather's business card:

M.L. Lipton, M.D.
Physician and Surgeon
Day or night, call 757-3535

I found nine cards like this and nine appointment cards with yellow edges. I reassembled the small stack and stuck it back in place.

In the next compartment was a single card with the following words written on the back in my grandfather's handwriting:

#141270
Vol 1 Page +3
Stub Volume 6795 page 20
Circuit Court
Champaign County
22 Sept 1913

Maybe this referred to the Lipstein family naturalization in Champaign, Illinois. I slid this card back in its appointed pocket and continued my search. In the next slot were membership and credit cards: *Master Charge*—good thru 06/68 | *Chevron National* Credit Card—we appreciate having served you since 1950. Good through OCT 1968 | *Smith's California*—The Largest Men's and Boy's Stores West of Chicago |

Atlantic Richfield—Preferred 13 year Customer | *A T & T Telephone* Credit Card 1968—Immediately say to the Operator–My credit card number is: J 757-3535 167 | Social Security No. 551-70-4193 | 1968 *American Medical Association* Active membership Card—AMA Convention-1968 San Francisco June 16-20 | *California Board of Medical Examiners* Certificate —Lipton, Morris L–Physician and Surgeon-Ronald Reagan–Governor -Void after February 28, 1970 | 1968 *California Medical Association* Membership Card | Membership Card for the *National Automobile Club* —Expiration Date 09 14 68. Member 19 Years | Membership in the *Alameda-Contra Costa Medical Association*—Civil Defense Assignment: As needed. Date of Issue: 12/1/67.

I found an Active Member card for the *Rotary Club of Antioch*, California— Medicine–Industrial Practice–Dues paid to 6/30/68. On the back I found a jubilant and boisterous signature. Morrie was a proud and joyful Rotarian.

The last thing was a folded paper, a *State of California* License to Carry Concealed Pistol, Revolver or Other Firearm

> Name: LIPTON, Morris L., MD
> Address: 200 20th Street Antioch, California
> Birthdate: 6-5-05
> Hgt: 5/9
> Wgt: 195
> Color Eyes: blu
> Color Hair: gry
> Desc. of Weapon–Manufacturer: S&W–Model: Rev
> Caliber: .39 - Serial No: 958623JW

Everything was frozen in 1968. The contents of the wallet provided a freeze-frame glimpse of 1968, when everything stopped for Morrie. All these things of life came to a halt when Morrie died, nothing to renew, no more Rotary Club dues to pay, no need to reapply for the license to carry a concealed weapon, no problem letting the credit cards expire.

I closed the wallet, took one more deep breath of the leather smell, and then tucked this artifact back in the cardboard box on the floor.

At my feet I had the distilled liquors of lifetimes and generations, condensed and collected in two cardboard boxes. I spent hours filtering through pictures and papers. I unpacked the boxes and cried at letters written by my grandfather, from the overseas war to his wife and young sons. I packed the stuff away again, feeling drained by the hard emotions.

At sporadic intervals through the weeks, I opened the boxes again and found my grandmother's medical records; charts, chronicles of pain. Cringing, I flipped through and learned things about my grandmother's body that I never wanted to know.

I found pictures of young women, young men and children who have all grown older: my ancestors, my father, and my uncles. I found unidentified black and white photos, hand-scrawled letters, typewriter strikeovers on thin airmail paper, diplomas, and birth, death, marriage, and baptismal certificates.

Put it away. Sifting and straining through lifetimes packed in cardboard boxes is tiring. Put it away for now.

The one thing I didn't pack away was the picture of my great grandmother, Rose. Instead, I propped her up on my desk. Her face seemed content and she smiled at me in quiet approval, giving a silent nod to my endeavors.

CHAPTER 2

SECRETS

My parents gave great power to their secrets. I'll never forget the evening I learned about their secret child. It was June 1995, and I was thirty-two years old. At that time, I lived in the same house and town I do now, Crockett, California. Funky, historical, hysterical Crockett happens to be four hundred and eight miles North of La Habra, where my parents lived at that time in Orange County.

Orange County is a mostly white, right-wing part of Southern California. When my little nuclear family visited down there, the Clinton/Gore sticker from 1992 that was still stuck on our van blinked like a beacon of our liberal bent. The street in La Habra where my folks lived was plain, with a boring, suburban sameness. Trimmed shrubs and cropped lawns didn't hide the run-down dumpiness of some of the older ranch-style homes. Strip malls with donut shops and nail salons lined the route to get to E. Francis Street in La Habra. On that unimaginative street, in a basic house, lived Theresa Lipton, my Native-Plant-Society, organic mother with her irrepressible energy, and Paul Lipton, my fair, analytical, and discriminating dad.

This Orange County place was a universe away from Berkeley in the 1960's where we lived on Virginia Street when I was a kid. It was a universe away from the hippy culture that was all around me as a kid, informing my world-view.

My folks were renting the house in La Habra so my dad could finish a few more years with Chevron and get full retirement benefits after his long career. The distance separating Crockett and La Habra made it difficult for my folks to see their grandkids as often as they would have liked. Jack Shaw was three years old. Carolyn Shaw was about four months old.

Kennan and I had been together for ten years by that time. We'd bought the Victorian-era house in Crockett a couple of years earlier and we already had two kids and a mortgage. We decided it was time to get hitched, and were in the midst of planning to be married on our front porch in September, 1995. The wedding would be a potluck barbeque. Friends and family would share the food and music and see us get married. Our wedding invitations were homemade and had an antique picture of the last segment of the 1927 Carquinez Bridge being lifted into place to complete the span. The invitation had the words: "Joined, finally."

The house in Crockett looked a lot like the A-frame, blue-gray house on Virginia Street in Berkeley. Both houses are old, north facing, with steep-pitched red composite shingle roofs. I came to realize that the blue-gray paint I chose for the exterior of the Crockett house was an unconscious psychological choice to mimic the look of the Berkeley house. The tall ceilings felt like the ceilings of my childhood that I stared up at before I went to sleep.

Crockett in the 1990s was still irreverent and renegade like Berkeley was in the 1960s and early 1970s. Crockett has a mix of artist warehouse studio spaces, terraced older homes on the hillside; old Italian families who have buildings named after them; young families with kids who love the small community, and blue-collar sugar workers. If it weren't for the biker vibe and the occasional Meth lab bust, you'd almost think you were in an idyllic factory town from the 1930s or 40s. Step on the cracks of the 1940 WPA sidewalks in Crockett and touch the history of the New Deal.

The brick sugar refinery has been running since 1906 and stands as a behemoth, with the neon sign that flashes "C & H Pure Cane Sugar" at the cars that approach the Carquinez Bridge heading east on Interstate 80.

I love and hate Crockett for all its lawlessness and history, the loud sounds of industry, the steam horn from the factory, the rattle and blare of the trains and the rare bellow of a foghorn. On Wednesdays and Sundays the town still smells like burnt sugar, caramelized molasses crackling in the air. Steam still pumps out of the old stack.

In 2006, the town of Crockett celebrated C&H Sugar, One Hundred Years of Sweetness 1906-2006. The centennial of the Sugar Plant made me think about my place in this century.

From our house in Crockett, we can see silent ships pass in front of our window; sometimes a colorful regatta dots the water. Even an occasional whale or two has ventured from the Pacific through the Bay to the Carquinez Strait and up into the Sacramento River Delta. My life has been lived along this waterway.

The life I understood was about to be altered by a phone call from my dad.

Kennan handed me the phone.

"It's your dad." It was late spring and early evening, still bright, and the big orange-pink sky touched San Pablo Bay just outside the living room window.

"Hi, Dad, how are you doing?"

"Hi, Cindy, we're fine. Everything is okay. Your mother and I have something important to tell you."

"Okay?"

"I think Mom wants to tell you herself. Here she is. Therese, come and talk to Cindy."

My mom came on the phone. She was nervous and her tone, hesitant. She hemmed and hawed and started and paused and swallowed and cleared her throat. Then, she got the words out, and I listened, dumbstruck.

"Thirty-five years ago, your dad and I had a baby and we gave it up for adoption. So you have a sister. She just got in touch with us."

The news didn't quite register, but I responded.

"Really? That's great. I always wanted a sister."

"You're not mad at us?"

"No, why would I be mad? It's great. Did she call you?"

"Your father talked to her first. Here, I'll put him on and he can answer your questions. I'm so glad you're not mad at us."

My mom handed the phone back to my dad. I was stunned, numb. So I listened.

"Hi, Cindy, a couple of days ago we got a call from a woman named Debbie Beth Silverblatt in Pennsylvania. At first, I thought she was a telemarketer and I was ready to hang up. Then she asked, 'Is this the Paul Lipton who gave up a baby for adoption in Pittsburgh, Pennsylvania in 1960?' I paused for a moment and then I said, 'yes'."

I continued to listen, speechless.

"She said she has had our names for a few years. She found out about us when the records were opened in 1983 and she got a copy of her birth certificate. Our names were listed on the birth certificate. She said she wasn't ready to call until now."

"So she is both of yours, you and Mom? Right?"

"Yes, both of ours. Then the next thing she asked me was, 'Do you have any idea where my mother is?'"

"She really asked that?" I absorbed what I could as my dad continued his measured explanation.

"Yes, she said. 'Do you have any idea where my mother is?' I said,

'Yeah, she's asleep on the sofa.'"

I cringed and laughed at that; some pretty heavy thoughts were going through my head. To think that they had a baby together, after they were married and gave it up. I guess it makes sense that that child would be surprised to find her birth parents' marriage intact so many years later. There must be a million reasons a kid makes up in her mind about why her parents had to give her up.

"Why did you do it, Mom?"

"It was the 1950s."

That answer never satisfied me, but since I was raised to be tolerant and accepting, I tried to respect their decision even though I didn't understand it.

"So she's Jewish? I have a Jewish sister?'

"Yes, we purposely wanted the baby to go to a Jewish family. We arranged the adoption through a lawyer and a Jewish adoption agency."

This I understood better than the 1950s answer. Even though we weren't technically, ethnically Jewish, we had Jewish ancestry, and my parents felt that a Jewish family would have like-minded values, and would have the resources to offer the baby a good standard of living and a good education.

For all the years of my life to that point, I had never known I had a sister. I had to get used to the idea that a person existed who shared both of my parents, a full-blooded sibling that Paul and Theresa had put up for adoption 35 years before.

I remember visiting my parents at their house in La Habra. Debbie was still on the East Coast, and the most of the communications were by phone. My mom talked with Debbie, in the kitchen, with the sliding pocket door closed.

When I looked at pictures of Debbie, I was struck by how her features resembled my mother's with a freakish uncanny precision. It seemed like I was looking at a younger version of Mom. Debbie's eyebrows and chin looked the same as Mom's.

Debbie had a son named Forrest, who was a few months younger than Jack. I felt relieved that Jack had been born first. Somehow it was important to have delivered the first grandchild.

After the revelation and reconciliation between the long-lost child and her parents, I had to stomach my mom's private, whispered conversations with Debbie. My mom would tell me that she shared things with Debbie that she had never shared with me. I felt like I'd been plopped in the middle of the parable of the prodigal child, whose homecoming was celebrated with the fatted calf, while the dutiful child who stayed, was left to the side. I cringed when the door would close on their private conversations and I was left on the outside.

Then Paul and Theresa moved back up to Northern California and Debbie and Forrest came out from the East Coast. Our parents agreed to let Debbie and Forrest stay for a while at their new house in Berkeley.

Visits felt uneasy. Why did Debbie seem like such a stranger? She seemed to want to feel at home, but she didn't know how to move about my parents house –- how to transition from a guest to a family member.

This phase soon passed into Debbie and Mom grinding against one another, as iron sharpeneth iron, so a man sharpeneth the countenance of a friend. They shared many interests in common, and prominent personality traits began to rub against tender feelings.

The biggest mistake turned out to be Debbie staying in our parents' house, unfamiliar with the unspoken customs. These customs are natural to family members who have eaten at the same table and slept under the same roof and walked the same floors for years and decades. The objects and the stories are familiar. But when a stranger that looked so much like us walked in, we made a visceral assumption that she should know the Lipton ways. But how could she? There's not a chromosome that remembers when we traveled to Brannan Island and fished for catfish in the Delta. There's not a chromosome that remembers which bowl is used for macaroni and cheese.

In September, 1995, at my wedding on the porch and barbeque potluck that followed, Uncle David said to my sister Debbie, "Well, you look like a Lipton."

"No I don't. I look like myself." To David's ears, Debbie's tone sounded militant; he shrugged and left her alone.

In the flurry of feelings on my wedding day, surrounded by all my best people, I had no appetite, but I did want to taste the potluck fare. So, I made myself a plate for later and stuck it in the fridge, uncovered. When the guests had departed, I planned to sit in a quiet place with my plate and enjoy.

My mother was frantic as she tidied the kitchen and told me that Debbie still had issues. I said it wasn't a good time to discuss it, but we'd talk later, and she could tell me everything that was going on. I heard that Debbie had highlighted passages in a book about adoptees and orphans called, "The Primal Wound."

Some issues take longer to resolve.

Later, when I went to retrieve the plate of food I had squirreled away, it was gone. My mother, who never wastes food, had thrown it out to make space in the fridge for leftovers.

CHAPTER 3

THE GOLEMANS AND THE LIPTONS

—

The Golemans and Liptons are related through my Jewish grandfather, Morrie. Morrie Lipstein and Irving Goleman were cousins. Back in 1932, Fay Weinberg married Irving Goleman. At that time, Morrie welcomed Fay to the family in this letter.

From Morrie to Irving and Fay Goleman

August 1, 1932

Chicago, Ill.

Dear Cousins,

Irving has always been my favorite cousin and <u>friend</u>. Therefore, by benefit of clergy and a good wholesome liking engendered by the few occasions we met you Fay, you are now our favorite "Cousiness" with all the rights and privileges pertaining thereto. Irving will inform you on the privileges!

Fran and I are both very happy that you are married and we wish to extend our congratulations to Irving. I'm not so sure you

made such a wonderful bargain Fay—for after all, Irving has

Lipstein blood in him.

Enclosed is a little gift which we hope you can use to good

advantage and which we send to you with best wishes and lots of

love.

—Morrie and Fran

The letter was written on stationery from Northwestern University, McKinlock Campus, Chicago, Illinois. In the bottom corner of the paper, in Fay's handwriting, was a note of explanation about Fran:

Morris Lipton's first wife. No children.

Sixty three years later, in the spring of 1995, Irving's widow, Fay invited the Lipton family to attend a Passover Seder at her home in Stockton.

The Seder table was full of strange foods like gefilte fish and chicken soup with matzo balls. Some of the fare was tasty, some flat and unenticing. The ritual was interesting to my Gentile, mostly Atheist family. We watched the working through of the Passover questions, the prayers, the bitter herbs.

The table was full of loved ones: Fay's daughter, Judy Goleman and her daughter Rachel; my favorite uncle, Dan; my cousin, Catherine; her baby, Duncan; my mom and dad, my little nuclear family consisting of myself, my husband Kennan, our 3-year-old son Jack, and our teeny-tiny 2-month-old baby Carolyn.

Throughout the evening, the Golemans made speeches, prayers and proclamations. While we ate, our hostess, Fay Goleman, stood up, all four-foot-ten of her smiling, wrinkled, wisdom and said, "You know what the Jews say the greatest sin is?" The room went silent. We all stopped chewing and looked at Fay as she finished her pronouncement, "…the Jews say the greatest sin is not living up to your potential."

When Fay said that, my Atheist, Gentile mother almost choked on her matzo. My dad had to whack her on the back with three firm, loving blows to dislodge the unleavened bread from her throat. Mom swallowed, smiled in embarrassment and covered her mouth with her napkin.

"Ah, Jeezus Christ Almighty," my mom muttered to me as if Jeezus would help her out on this one. No effing way, since she hadn't baptized her kids or sent them to college, much to the chagrin of my devout Catholic grandmother, Martha Pigati, and my Atheist intellectual grandmother, Mildred Lipton.

Grandma Pigati even kept a very special bottle of champagne and promised to open it when we kids were baptized, but this incentive never worked on my mom, and we remained pagan babies.

Now, here we were at a Jewish Seder as the grandmothers turned in their graves with sin and chagrin from every side. I gave an extra sinful smirk when my 3-year-old, unbaptized, uncircumcised, Gentile son found the Afikomen to the squeals of delight of the elders. The feast and the speeches rolled on.

No one in my family has a college degree, not my dad, my mom, my brother, my husband or me. I have found a term to describe my family and myself. We are autodidacts.

"Why is this night different from every other?"

It's the night I realized the Lipton family is a powerful brand of sinners.

A few years ago, when I developed an interest in herbs and essential oils, my dad made a distillation apparatus for me so I could distill my own.

My homemade still was an old pressure cooker pot, a cooling condenser, tubing and a re-circulating pump from a garden fountain. The idea is to boil water along with the flowers or herbs on the stove. The steam rises up into the coiled copper condenser, where it is cooled by the re-circulating water. The steam re-condenses into liquid as the steam cools, including the volatile aromatic oils from the plants.

The sweet-smelling liquor is collected and the essential oil is separated from the water fraction using a glass separatory funnel. The oil floats to the top and you let the water layer out the bottom through a stopcock, like a tap, and you are left with the oil. The most precious and expensive oil is Rose Otto.

When my great grandmother, Rose Vogel, was a girl, she was photographed with her older sister, Cecilie. Some years later, circa 1903, both Rose and Cecilie appear with their spouses in the Vogel family portrait taken in Konigsberg.

The grand matriarch, Ida Vogel sits in the center of the picture surrounded by her well-dressed and affluent clan. Ida's facial features look primitive; her angular cheekbones are almost Neanderthal. Standing behind Ida is Rose, my most precious and dear great grandmother. My great grandfather, Herman stands beside Rose, and flashes a rakish smile from the portrait. From the smirk on his face, I can see he was a man of personality.

Rose wears Victorian white, delicate and vulnerable. The more I have learned about her, the more I realize that on the inside, Rose was a force of nature, a political, social, and cultural being. And Rose was devoted to Herman.

Testimony of the Rose's devotion to Herman is the square locket, that I found 100 years later inside the ragged leather case that held her pearlescent opera glasses. In this personal and intimate hiding place, she kept him forever. Now, I keep both Rose and Herman in that same locket close to my heart.

Rose's locket found its way to me as heirlooms do, by a magic chance happening. One evening, at my parent's house in Berkeley, the family was sitting around the round oak table that was extended to oblong with several wooden leaves. I don't remember what we were talking about that made my mother pull the leather case from the cabinet. Mom reached in and removed Rose's Victorian opera glasses from the case.

"Hey, there's something else in here." Mom fished in the bottom of the case and pulled out a square locket, old, like a miniature book. When she opened it, she found a picture of Rose on one side and Herman on the other. Mom passed it to me so I could have a look. It was tarnished and a tiny jewel was chipped out.

"I need this," I said.

"No, you don't get that yet," my dad said.

Ignoring my father's senseless veto, my mother said, "What are you going to do with it?"

"I'm going to wear it."

"Okay, you can have it."

My great grandmother's locket finding its way to me was as though she wanted me to know her and to tell the story of our family the best I could. Her DNA is in my bones and I wear her image on a chain, close to my heart, as my treasure and my heirloom.

Rose and Herman were young once, a couple in love, but as the years passed, they suffered misfortune and loss. They lost a daughter named Jenny and their movie theater burned. Herman left a residual sense of sadness. He was my dear, dejected, tragic and handsome great grandfather. I keep coming back to the photo that shows Herman when he was older, his stooped form walking in a Chicago Park in the 1920s. The picture is labeled Pa.

Herman was the only boy among six sisters. He had three older sisters: Ida, Fannie and Goldie, and three younger sisters, Bertha, Anna and Della. I call them the Seven Siblings Lipstein, and I imagine each one standing on one of the Seven Bridges of Konigsberg waiting for the mythic lovers to cross over each bridge, once, and once only, as they wander to and from Kniephoff Island. But this is not possible.

The Seven Bridges of Konigsberg is a famous historical problem in mathematics. The solution by Leonhard Euler in 1735 is considered the birth of Graph Theory, which later led to the idea of topology. Euler proved it impossible to cross each bridge only once and represented the proof topographically.

Before the Seven Siblings Lipstein came to this city of knowledge and enlightenment, Konigsberg had its own great thinker, Immanuel Kant, whose seminal phrase I clutch and hold and shove deep in my pocket as my legacy, *Sapere aude*—Dare to Know.

The Enlightenment spread and many Lithuanian Jews became devotees of the Haskala, the Jewish Enlightenment movement in Eastern Europe. And the most enlightened taste buds, from Lithuania, Latvia and Russia preferred the peppery gefilte fish. Jews living farther west, including most of Poland, Germany and the rest of Western Europe preferred the sweet gefilte fish.

The Litvaks are proud to claim that many leading academics, scientists and philosophers are of Lithuanian Jewish descent. I am proud to share my Litvak heritage with Peggy Lipton of the Mod Squad; the Three Stooges - Moe, Shemp and Curly; folksinger, Bob Dylan; the Beatles Manager, Brian Epstein; the painter, Marc Chagall; the singer-songwriter, Leonard Cohen, and Menachem Begin, the Israeli Prime Minister from 1977-1983. I like to think we all share a taste for the peppery gefilte fish.

Ida Lipstein was the eldest of the Seven Siblings and she grew up and married Abraham Goldman. Somehow, the name Goldman morphed into Goleman. Ida was the matriarch of the esteemed Goleman clan and mother of Professor Irving Goleman, the first cousin to my grandfather Morrie.

The Seven Siblings all left Konigsberg near the end of the 1800s, near the turn of the 20th Century. I don't know whether they retreated from the Pale of Settlement, or from pogroms against the Jews, or from the May Laws that restricted by quota the number of Jews that could enter University. The Russian economy was troubled, so it makes sense that this was the time to make the move to a new place. America held the promise of financial and educational opportunity; what more could the Jews want?

I have the idea that my family heard the Statue of Liberty call out, "Give me you rich, educated Jews, yearning to get a good education and make a good living in this land of opportunity."

In 1907, Rose, with two-year-old Morris on her hip, boarded the SS Kaiser Wilhelm der Grosse heading for New York Harbor.

In about 1908, in Chicago, Rose and Herman had a baby daughter named Jenny. Young Morris pushed his sister in a stroller and cared for her. The year was 1909 or 1910, and Jenny died. I don't know why.

By 1911 or 1912, Herman and Rose ran the Varsity Theater in Champaign, Illinois. The Varsity had opened in 1906 as a Nickelodeon and later became a silent movie cinema. This period of time comes into some focus as it is told in this letter from my grandfather's brother, my great uncle Al:

𝒻ROM AL LIPTON TO PAUL LIPTON

November 15, 1990
Dallas, Tx.

Dear Paul and all the California Liptons:
. . . In regard to your questions: My father Herman came from Nisni-Novgorod [probably misspelled] from one of the Baltic Republics, Lithuania I believe. He was an only son, but had 6 sisters, one of whom was Irving Goleman's mother... One of the other sister's families lived in South Africa. They started the first movie house there... My dad Herman was well-educated, spoke about 7 languages and also studied dentistry in Europe. However, after he and my mother and Morris came to America in about 1906 or 7, he had trouble making a living. He did translation and book-keeping. Also worked as a salesman and operated the "Varsity" movie house in Champaign, Ill, where I was born. The film used in those days was very inflammable, couldn't get fire insurance and it burned down in about 1916 and we moved to Chicago.

Although the Varsity Theater was damaged in the fire and my great grandparents left Champaign for Chicago, the theater continued on in a series of incarnations. Sound films began playing there in the late 1920s. In 1943, the Varsity was remodeled and renamed the Rex Theater, advertised as fireproof when it opened its doors to reveal new leather seats, air-conditioning and a crème and blue color scheme. The place seated 330 and was decorated in the Art Moderne style. The first movie shown at the Rex was the film "Iceland" with Sonia Henie.

In 1948, the proprietor renamed the theater the Illini, and began to show art and foreign films. From 1963 to 1966, the place was called the Encore for a short time, but in 1966 the name changed back to the Illini and in 1968 started playing adult features. The Illini closed down in 1983.

In 1987, a church purchased the building and held services and revivals there for 10 years until the church moved out. Today, the theater operates as a live music club and bar called the Highdive.

What a long strange trip.

After fire destroyed the Varsity Theater, Herman had to find a new way to make a living. In 1920, the U.S. Census listed Herman Lipstein's occupation as an advertising man for the stockyards, the Chicago stockyards. Not so many years before, Upton Sinclair had been an eyewitness and a journalist documenting the sad conditions of the workers in the Chicago Stockyards.

The Jungle was required reading. The story told of an immigrant family that suffered immeasurable tragedy. Sinclair's goal as a Socialist

writer was to shine light on the beef industry and the slave wages and
inhumane conditions endured by the workers on the killing floors.
Instead, *The Jungle* caused an outrage and a muck-raking uproar about
the purity and safety of America's meat supply. This was 1906, when the
Pure, Food and Drug Act was passed by Congress and signed into law by
Theodore Roosevelt.

Sinclair said later: "I aimed at the public's heart, and by accident I hit
it in the stomach."

By 1930, my great grandmother Rose was listed as Head of
Household in the census. My Grandpa Morris already had his Pharmacy
degree and was studying to be a M.D. while his first wife, Francis,
worked as a stenographer in a law office. Grandpa's brother, Albert, was a
demonstrator of toilet articles, a salesman I suppose.

Herman was gone. I heard he died of diabetes.

As Rose aged, she became a wire whisk of a woman, delicate
and small-boned with a small face, dark bushy eyebrows and white hair.
Strong-minded and idealistic, she expressed a continual wish for an
egalitarian future. Rose Lipton signed her letters with hope that there
would be "Peace and Equality for all Mankind."

It was important to Rose that each of her sons be educated and
make a good living in a professional occupation. Rose was proud that her
older son, Morris, was a medical doctor and her younger son, Albert, was
an engineer.

Morrie and Al both married nice Jewish girls. But later, Morrie fell in love with an Italiana, a shikseh. I don't know the circumstances of the breakup of my grandfather from his first wife, but I know he fell in love with my grandmother, Mildred Formento, in the 1930s in Chicago.

Such is life for the Jewish mother.

I wish there were more pieces of Rose left, more pictures of her, more objects she touched and more words she wrote. I was too late to meet her in life, but I have her handwriting in letters and her face in the locket, beside the face of Herman Lipstein, her love and her husband.

Great Grandmother Rose Vogel's family in Konigsberg ca. 1903. Back row standing left to right: Cecilie's husband Karpas, Heinrich Vogel, Sr., Herman Lipstein, Rose Lipstein neé Vogel, Heinrich Vogel, Jr., Heinrich Jr.'s wife (maybe Louisa). Front row seated left to right: Cecilie Karpas, baby Dora Karpas, unknown boy, Ida Vogel, the matriarch (pictured below in the striped dress).

Heinrich Sr. and Ida Vogel, my great-great grandparents ca. 1870s.

Vogel siblings ca. 1882. Heinrich, Jr., Cecilie, and Rose seated on the right, with her feet nicely crossed.

Sisters Rose and Cecilie Vogel ca. late 1880s.

Rose Vogel as a young woman ca. 1900.

Roses's older sister Cecilie Vogel as a young woman ca. 1900.

Karpas family ca. 1903. Cecilie, her husband, and daughter Dora.

Left: Great Grandfather Herman Lipstein as a young man. He was the only son, and had six sisters—three older and three younger.

Below: Four of the six Lipstein sisters: Ida, Goldie, Fannie, and Bertha.

*My Great Grandparents
Herman and Rose Lipstein as a
handsome young couple,
ca 1903.*

*Herman and Rose dressed for
the opera, ca 1905. I wonder
if she had her opera glasses and
locket by this time.*

Cousins left to right: Dora Karpas, Albert Lipstein, and Morris Lipstein.

Morrie Lipstein and his baby sister Jenny, who died.

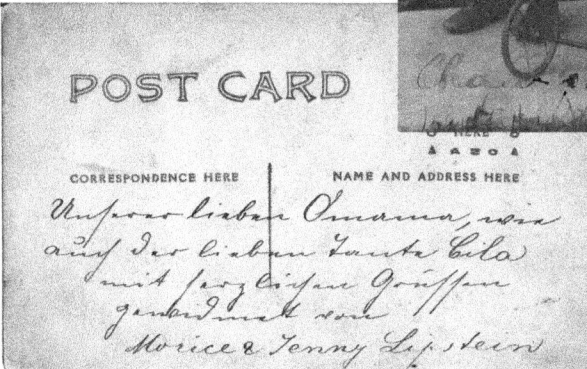

Formento kids left to right: Rose, Michael, my grandma Mil Formento. Chicago ca. 1914

Isabella with all four Formento kids left to right: Mil, Mike, Violet and Rose (nice bowl haircuts). Chicago ca. 1918

My grandma Mil looks like a puppet the way Isabella is holding her. Left to right: Mildred, Isabella, and Rose Formento and Isabella's mother Angelina Del Re. Chicago ca. 1911.

Above: Formento family, Chicago ca. 1915. Left to right Paul, Rose, Violet, Mil (on a chair), and Isabella.

Isabella and the dog smiling on the steps in Chicago ca. 1918.

Herman Lipstein, Union Park, Chicago, Illinois, 1924
This photo was labeled "Pa" by Grandpa Morrie. This is
the last photo that we have of Herman.

CHAPTER 4

THIRD COUSIN TO A BESTSELLER

I am convinced that if I had been raised by Jews and had had a Bat Mitzvah, I would be accomplished and acclaimed and published by now. I was already 30 before I even knew about my famous third cousin, Naomi Wolf. I felt puny next to her expansive accomplishments. Naomi had written several books, including the bestseller *The Beauty Myth*, and she was a figure in the Third Wave of Feminism. I had seen her numerous times on television, but had only met her at a book signing. She inscribed my copy of *The Beauty Myth* with:

"10/18/92. For Cindy, Love and hope, Naomi Wolf. So glad to find my cousins."

Years later, in 2008, my dad didn't understand why I volunteered to drive Naomi and her kids from SFO to Stockton, but my mom did. It was my chance to get to know this accomplished branch of the family, the Golemans. The tribe flows from the riverhead Fay Goleman, who came into my life as a generational touch point and a strong peripheral figure.

She is both a funny duck and a matriarch, whose clan casts the dazzling glare of accomplishment in the squinting covered eyes of the Liptons.

I am ambivalent about my relationship to my Jewish heritage, and to the extended family that casts a mighty shadow on what the Liptons have not done. My analog in the alternate universe of the Golemans is Naomi Wolf. Naomi represents my more accomplished self. She was born the year before me in San Francisco. Her dark thick hair and blue eyes make her stand out; striking in comparison to my thin dishwater blond-brown stringy hair and hazel eyes, a muddy mix that gives away my Jewish-Italian gene pool.

Naomi is my counter-ego. I come from the Gentile, peasant off-shoot of the family and Naomi comes from the blueblood, Jewish branch. I was born on the mutt-end of a Jewish dynasty.

So it happened that on Saturday, November 29, 2008, I was a tree standing steady and rooted while leaves and sticks and brambles whipped around me, blown every which way. So it goes with the Goleman's.

Fay Goleman would be turning 98 on Sunday, and her far-flung tribe was planning to gather to celebrate at her home in Stockton. I hadn't been to the Stockton house since 1995, to the Seder 13 years before. In some twist of circumstances, I was recruited to pick up Naomi from SFO. I was given scanty details, but I figured I was resourceful enough to figure it out.

Earlier in the week, I had left a message for Naomi saying that I was her ride to Fay's birthday party. When Naomi called me back, the cell phone connection was bad. As I fumbled with my hands-free earpiece, she waited and then she said, "May I speak now?" What a forceful woman. She proceeded to explain to me what she thought I needed to know, neither of us realizing I was less informed or caught up with the plan than she was. I convinced her that I would be there to meet her and the children at the airport and that she didn't need to cancel her plans to join the celebration.

I clarified that her kids Rosa and Joey were coming from Portland, Oregon where they had been with their dad, David Shipley for Thanksgiving. Naomi was coming from New York on the red-eye and somehow we would all meet up at SFO and I would drive them to Stockton.

I was right on time Saturday, and as I spiraled through the SFO parking garage, David Shipley called to say that the kids' plane was stuck on the ground and their flight would be late. Later I looked up David Shipley on the Internet and I learned from Wikipedia that he worked for President Bill Clinton from 1995 to 1997 as Special Assistant to the President and Senior Presidential Speechwriter. It said that he was born in Portland, Oregon, in 1963 and that he has two children with former wife Naomi Wolf; they divorced in 2005. So here I was picking up David Shipley's former wife and two children.

Fast forward to everyone arriving and me waiting while Naomi gathered her brood, then to Naomi and I talking during the 100 mile drive from SFO to Stockton. The kids fell asleep and Naomi showed intense interest in my family relationships. We discussed the sister my parents gave up for adoption and she shared some of her own psychological theories and experiences. Naomi had also had a reunion with a half-brother whose existence had been hidden from her until a few years ago. This brother was the offspring of a woman at a Writer's Colony and her dad, Leonard Wolf, who comes into the story after we arrive in Stockton.

Wikipedia has the following entry for Leonard Wolf, "Leonard Wolf is an author, teacher, and the father of Naomi Wolf. He is known for his authoritative annotated versions of classic gothic horror novels, including *Dracula, Frankenstein, The Strange Case of Dr Jekyll and Mr. Hyde,* and *The Phantom of the Opera.* He was born in Vulcan, Romania, formerly called Transylvania."

The long drive gave us plenty of time to talk, and I felt the intensity of Naomi's questions.

"How is the relationship between your sister and your parents now?"

"A rift developed between them when my dad insisted that Debbie find her own place. I don't understand what my sister expected from them."

"There's a psychological concept called Deprived Entitlement, when I person feels entitled to something they needed, but didn't get." Naomi fell asleep in the passenger's seat of my Honda, as I drove the levee roads on the way through the Delta.

Fast forward again to the upstairs room in the old house in Stockton. Fay Goleman was a pink wisp in her bathrobe with white hair and high cheekbones. The bay windows threw a natural light on a circle of chairs where small groups of close family and friends took turns sitting with Fay and talking. She was very frail, but coherent, the brilliant wellspring that produced this Jewish intellectual dynasty.

I brought a card. I would not be attending the festivities the next day, but wanted to pay a small tribute to Fay. She read it.

"That's a wonderful card, I shall keep it." It said that she was a regular character in the letters my grandparents exchanged during WWII. I promised Fay I would make sure my grandparents letters were placed in a library somewhere. I was struck by Fay's graciousness.

I sat with Fay and related the contents of some of the letters. Fay's younger daughter Judith sat with us too. Judith is as loving and disheveled and effusive and scatterbrained as they come. We talked about a pair of lovebirds with pink cheeks that my grandparents had given to the Goleman girls in 1943. Judith remembered the birds and I remembered a picture of Judith as a little girl. In the picture, Judith's round, bright cheeks were just like the lovebirds.

A group of people burst into the room at that moment and hugs and greetings were passed around. Fay greeted the tall man who entered as Leonard, and it registered to me that this was Leonard Wolf, Naomi's dad.

Leonard was tall, maybe 6'4". From the discussions during the car ride, I already knew that he had fathered a child out of wedlock, and that he was the foremost expert on Dracula, and that he was 16 years older than his wife Deborah. Leonard and Deborah had flown in from New York City to Oakland and rode to Stockton with Aaron Wolf, Naomi's older brother.

Judith introduced me, "This is Cindy Lipton. She is related to us through Irving."

Leonard Wolf nodded a greeting, shook my hand and sat across from me. He asked Fay how she was feeling. Fay's response:

"I'm ninety-eight years old. It reminds of that poem you taught me Leonard."

Fay began to recite the verse, and Leonard joined in with his resounding voice.

> *From too much love of living,*
>
> *From hopes and fears set free,*
>
> *We thank with brief thanksgiving,*
>
> *Whatever gods may be,*
>
> *That no life lives forever,*
>
> *And dead men rise up never.*
>
> *And even the weariest river,*
>
> *Winds somewhere safe to sea.*

"Who wrote that, Leonard?"

"Swinburne", Leonard said, "a Victorian poet who was a master of metered verse until Walt Whitman came along with what was then known as free verse. At that time, the metered verse fell out of favor. That particular poem is about not believing in God. Tell me, dear Fay, what brings this verse to your mind today?"

Before she could answer, the room was spun into frenzy with the appearance of Aaron Wolf and his kids. They kissed their great grandmother and the conversation was swept into Aaron's adventures and resourceful escape from Laos to be able to join the family.

From where I was sitting, I had a clear view of why this poem was on Fay Goleman's mind, but her family did not venture anywhere near the idea of Fay dying. Fay was telling everyone in the room how weary she was. Even the weariest river winds somewhere safe to sea.

Rewind to SFO the morning of November 29th, where I was sitting, waiting for Naomi and her kids. My cell phone rang and it was a quasi-frantic call from Judith, the one with the cheeks of a lovebird.

"Cindy, does Naomi know if her brother Aaron got out of Laos? We can't call anyone, because everyone is on a plane right now. We need to know, because Deborah and Leonard are about to arrive in Oakland and Aaron was going to drive them to Stockton. If he's not there, we'll come out and pick them up."

"When Naomi gets here, I'll see what I can find out."

"Cindy, thank you. Today you're the hub of this family."

Naomi arrived soon after that and it was a flurry of confusion because of airline and gate mix-ups and last minute changes, which, I was beginning to learn, is the Goleman status quo.

I relayed the message from Judith and asked Naomi if Aaron had gotten out of Laos.

"Yes, he got out. I spoke to him. He's fine."

"Could you give Judith a call and let her know?"

"Mommy, tell us about Uncle Aaron."

"I'll tell you all in the car."

Driving out from SFO, Naomi shushed her kids off and on and then she gushed about San Francisco being the most beautiful city in the world. As we passed Sutro Tower, she pointed out the hills around Twin Peaks.

"See that hill, that's where Mommy grew up in a magical forest. Mommy will take you there some day." I soaked up all the interactions with fascination. Naomi continued,

"And we're going to pass a wind farm."

"You mean Altamont Pass? I was planning to go a different way."

"Oh, of course, go whichever way you're comfortable with."

"Mommy, can you tell us about Uncle Aaron, now?"

"Yes, Honey, yes. Mommy will tell you. So, Uncle Aaron was working on water projects in Laos, when the people of Thailand decided to rise up against the government, which is a really good thing, but just a hassle for people like Uncle Aaron, who were trying to fly out of the Bangkok airport. It took two days for Uncle Aaron to get out. He ended up renting a car and driving to Hanoi and bribing officials to get a flight.

But he did get out and he'll be driving Grandma and Grandpa to Fay's and we'll see him soon."

"Will his kids be there?"

"Yes, I think so."

Escape from Laos, just another typical hassle. We went through the Caldecott Tunnel and I showed Naomi the crosses on the hill at the Lafayette BART station. She approved of the war protest remembrance and we continued talking as the kids fell asleep in the back seat.

> BANGKOK, Thailand (CNN) --
> November 28, 2008
> On Friday, Bangkok's two main airports remained occupied by anti-government protesters from The People's Alliance of Democracy (PAD). The airports have been closed since Tuesday, stranding thousands of passengers and dealing a severe blow to the crisis-stricken Southeast Asian nation's economy at the height of the tourist season.

Aaron Wolf PhD has authored the following books: *A Purity of Arms: An American in the Israeli Army*; and *Core and Periphery: A Comprehensive Approach to Middle Eastern Water*.

Back to the upstairs room in Stockton, to the circle of chairs. Leonard Wolf was there, Aaron Wolf had bounded in from Laos with his little boy, and Naomi's son Joey trailed after his cousin.

Judith announced that Fay was holding court, and one of the boys stood up tall and spoke out loud,

"Order in the court! I am the Chief Justice," resulting in adult laughter. How Jewish is that? Little kids role-playing as characters from the Judicial System.

There I was, in the middle of this joyous and intimate family gathering, feeling both out of place and welcome at the same time. Next thing I knew, a woman was standing next to me, squeezing my hand in greeting and looking into my face with a probing expression. I was surprised by the focused intensity of attention she showed. It took me a few moments to deduce who she was. Her reddish hair confounded me. In all the pictures I'd ever seen, Deborah Goleman was a dark-haired child or a brunette young woman.

My first impression of Deborah was that she was energetic, wiry, strident and bossy. So here I was with the Goleman sisters, Deborah and Judith in their natural habitat. I could see that Judith was accommodating, and that Deborah was in control. It was easy to see where Naomi got some of her traits. Bossiness and intensity were her maternal birthright.

As the day progressed, I joined the Goleman women in the preparations for the feast; take-out pizza devolved into to-go plates from Applebee's. Judith and Deborah were comfortable with my presence; they were the only ones who knew who I was, how I was connected. They grew up with my dad and uncles; they knew my grandparents Morrie and Mil, and my great grandmother Rose.

Before we ate we all held hands in a big circle and the Golemans sang praises and made proclamations of thankfulness.

Naomi asked me, "Do you feel like you're Jewish?"

"Well, I can't be Jewish because my mother's not Jewish."

"Yeah, I know. I'm really sorry about that."

"Why are you sorry about Jewish Law?"

"It's just so exclusive and patriarchal."

I shrugged as we continued dishing out food.

Later, I ran an errand with Deborah and on the way back she pointed out the University of the Pacific and talked about how both of her parents, Fay and Irving Goleman, had been professors. Then she navigated me to a particular house, on a street in the neighborhood.

"I only went out with this guy because of his house. You'll see why."

As I pulled up, I saw what looked like a New Orleans mansion, transplanted from St. Charles Avenue to Stockton, California.

"He was such a WASP, but the house is unbelievable."

Later, Deborah and I went for a walk and she told me about her father, Irving. She spoke of him as being distant, inaccessible. He disapproved of Deborah's relationship with Leonard Wolf. Irving died before Naomi was born and Deborah believes that Naomi embodies him. She showed me the park and the pond where she and my dad used to hang out as teenagers. She agreed that my great grandmother, Rose, was speaking to me and was thrilled that I was making contact with my ancestors. The most profound thing Deborah Goleman shared with me was something about my grandfather, Morrie Lipton.

"You know, Morrie knew I was already pregnant with Aaron when

Leonard and I got married."

"How did he know?"

"Well, he was a doctor. And we just had that kind of bond."

When I got home from this sojourn into the Goleman world, I began to wonder more about how we were connected. It was through Irving, Deborah's father. I knew very little about Irving, but somehow this figure of a man was leaving an impression on my mind. He wasn't quite intruding, but pressing me to consider him, to consider his life and existence. I was curious. I found a brief article in which a former student relates this experience about Professor Irving Goleman. The professor would make the following profession in class.

Who am I?

I am an idealist whose credo is:

I believe that God is good and not a monster or the devil, and that He needs our help.

I believe there is a genius in every human being.

CHAPTER 5

TRICKSTER

—

I harvested sprigs of rosemary from my backyard bush and cranked up my home still for the first time. I put water in the pot along with the rosemary, fit the lid to the pot and put the pot on the stove. I clamped the condenser to a stand, attached all the tubing to the condenser and pump, and set the fire burning under the pot. The steam rose and the cold water circulated through the copper coil, cooling the steam until the condensate dripped into the collection vessel. A skimpy layer of oil floated to the top and I got a puny yield of rosemary oil.

The rosemary plant contains a lot of strong fragrant oil. I wanted to test the system on a plentiful and prolific specimen to begin with, because I knew it would take armloads and basketsful of rose petals to extract a few drops of Rose Otto.

I shopped around, researched the price of the precious oil and found Rose Otto from *Rosa damescena*, Damask Roses from the Valley of Roses in Bulgaria. I choked on the price-- 5 milliliters of Rose Otto cost \$125.00. From the same company, I could order 10 milliliters of Rosemary Oil from *Rosmarinus officinalis* for \$5.00.

That's because it takes sixty thousand roses to make an ounce of pure essential Rose Otto, sixty roses to make a single drop. How would I gather enough rose petals? Maybe I could wait until the season of bloom hit its peak, in late April or early May, and then I could raid the rose gardens in Berkeley and Oakland. Maybe I could scrounge around the back doors and dumpsters of florists or farmers markets or funeral homes.

Relics and remembrances of Rose Lipton, my great grandmother, are rare and dear. Where did her things go? I guess they were packed away when she moved into the convalescent hospital, but where did her things end up? Were there papers or correspondences? Did she save them or throw them away? How would I gather the armloads and basketsful of Rose remnants to distill a few drops? My mother doesn't know what happened to Grandma Rose's things. She thinks maybe Mil threw them away long ago.

"You know Mil throws stuff out."

"What do you remember about Rose?"

"I remember visiting Rose in her apartment in Antioch, by the Stamm Theater. She'd make tea ahead of time, really strong. Then later she'd dilute it and serve it."

My ancestor longing took root when I started to study Hoodoo Rootwork through a correspondence course. As I worked through the lessons and the homework assignments, I dug my own roots and collected the dirt that clung to them.

This is literal.

For Homework One, I was assigned to collect a folk belief, a story, or a saying from my family. The course is based on African-American folk magic, also called, "Hoodoo, or Voodoo, as it is pronounced by the whites," said Zora Neale Hurston.

So for Homework One, I told about the family custom to "knock on wood" to repel the Evil Eye, when I had just tempted Fate by saying something like, "I've got it made now." As soon as those words left my mouth, I thought better of dangling that bait in front of the jaws of Fate, so I had to follow with, "Knock on wood."

For Homework Four, the class was assigned to buy graveyard dirt. This practice is a form of contagious magic, a spiritual transaction with the dead. The dead and ancestors are venerated in many traditions and are called on to help folks solve their problems and fulfill their desires. And graveyard dirt is a powerful curio to do this work. For healing work, a person might collect dirt from the grave of a doctor. For protection, a soldier might be chosen.

In the Hoodoo tradition, dirt from the graves of loved ones and ancestors is powerful and intimate because they loved us in life. It is natural for a grandfather to help a granddaughter, for a mother to help her son.

I knew right where to go to get the dirt of my precedents. I didn't feel taboo or fear, as some students do when working on Homework Four. This communion with my ancestors in Memory Gardens felt natural and comfortable. I entered the cemetery through the front gate and parked my car on the circle drive. In one pocket, three silver Mercury dimes clinked against a pint of Ancient Age whiskey. In the other pocket, I'd stuffed a stack of three shot glasses wrapped in paper bags to collect the dirt.

I dug first from Rose, because she is the oldest ancestor I can touch. I imagined her dark eyes and white hair and a half-smile of earnest pleasure at my presence and my interest. I imagined holding her frail hand in both of mine and her approval washed over me.

I dug the dirt out with the shot glass until the glass fit in the hole, flush with the ground. Then I paid for the dirt with the silver dime and the whiskey by filling the glass to overflowing and letting the distilled spirits soak into her grave.

I did the same for my dear grandparents, Mildred and Morrie. As I acted out the ritual, I communed with them the best I could. I remembered them and I pictured them. I asked them to look out for me and to help me get what I wanted from life. I've got to believe my ancestor spirits have got my back.

I have always loved cemeteries and tombs and stones. When I visit a new place I like to see the burial sites and read the grave markers. Now I had discovered a way to go deeper. And I became fixated with the idea of collecting dirt from local literary figures.

The first famous dirt I bought was Ina Coolbrith, the literary mother of Jack London. I read a biography of Jack London's life and in this way got to know Ina.

Ina's mother had fled a plural Mormon marriage and married a newspaperman. The family had brought Ina, the first pioneer child overland into California. Ina established the Oakland Free Library where she met and mentored the young Jack London.

Ina was the first Poet Laureate of California. In Oakland, Ina raised the daughter of Joaquin Miller, a half Indian girl called Cali-Shasta. In San Francisco, Ina lost many of her writings in the 1906 Earthquake fire.

I learned where Ina was buried and decided to collect her dirt, gathering Ina to help me with my literary endeavors. I drove to the end of Piedmont Avenue in Oakland into the gates of Mountain View Cemetery. The map from the office led me to her place of interment.

I sat on Ina's grave and read her poem aloud,

> *When the grass shall cover me,*
> *Head to foot where I am lying;*
> *When not any wind that blows,*
> *Summer blooms nor winter snows,*
> *Shall awake me to your sighing:*
> *Close above me as you pass,*
> *You will say, "How kind she was,"*

You will say, "How true she was,"

-When the grass grows over me.

When the grass shall cover me,

Holden close to earth's warm bosom,

While I laugh, or weep, or sing

Nevermore, for anything.

You will find in blade and blossom,

Sweet small voices, odorous,

Tender pleaders in my cause,

That shall speak me as I was

— When the grass grows over me.

When the grass shall cover me!

Ah, beloved, in my sorrow

Very patient, I can wait,

Knowing that, or soon or late,

There will dawn a clearer morrow:

When your heart will moan "Alas!

Now I know how true she was;

Now I know how dear she was"

—When the grass grows over me!

Later I made a special box to contain Ina's grave dirt. I decorated it with copies of old photos of Ina, when she was a child and when she was a young woman, then middle-aged, and then very old with a lace kerchief over her head. Ina Coolbrith was Jack London's literary mother and I heard their correlated voices. I have the power of the human finger bone that I laid in Ina Coolbrith's graveyard dirt; the white phalanges against the dark soil represent the touch of the literary spiritual mother.

Disassembled relics from the past attract me, like the cat bones I found in the weeds along Crockett Boulevard behind the rail. I saw the bleached white vertebrae against the dry brush and dirt, and I sifted through and collected all the bones I could find. When I got them home, I sorted them and named them the best I could, femurs and ribs and scapulae, and a perfect five-fingered cat paw that looked like a tiny skeletal hand.

I have often visited the Bone Room in Albany on Solano Avenue. The place calls itself a Natural History Store and they sell everything from iridescent beetle wings to exotic feathers and shells, skulls with antlers to an articulated giraffe neck and head, mounted for display.

I went to the Bone Room to find a human finger bone. I looked through an assortment and matched three bleached phalanges, all three joints including the fingertip, and I purchased the finger. This finger rests in the box of Ina's graveyard dirt, signifying the touch of the literary mother.

Once upon a time, Jack London washed past my window. In John Barleycorn, Jack London's autobiographical sketch, London tells of falling into the same water that flows outside my Crockett window.

...after a prodigious drunk, I was tottering aboard a sloop at the end of the wharf... The tides sweep through the Carquinez Straits as in a mill-race, and the full ebb was on when I stumbled overboard... I was borne away by the current... in my inflamed condition the contact of the water with my skin soothed me like cool linen... I contented myself with floating and dreaming long drunken dreams. Before daylight, the chill of the water and the passage of the hours had sobered me sufficiently to make me wonder what portion of the Straits I was in... I could make out the Selby Smelter on the Contra Costa shore and the Mare Island lighthouse. I started to swim for the Solano shore, but was too weak and chilled, and made so little headway... And I knew fear. I was sober now, and I didn't want to die. I discovered scores of reasons for living. And the more reasons I discovered, the more liable it seemed that I was going to drown anyway... I knew the end was near. And then the boat came--a Greek fisherman running in for Vallejo; and again I had been saved...

Jack London is not the only wayward creature to float past my home. Numerous creatures and vessels have passed through the Carquinez Straits waterway in front of my window. I know of tugboats, tankers, barges, sea lions, sturgeons, not to mention Jack London and the Humpback whales.

In May 2007, a wayward mother Humpback and her calf had swum through the Golden Gate into San Francisco Bay. The pair turned right past Richmond and continued through San Pablo Bay, into the Carquinez Straits and up the river. No one knew why. The experts reported propeller wounds on the mother whale. For all the efforts of the Coast Guard to lure or drive them back to sea, the cetaceous pair lingered. During her sojourn, the injured mother whale was harpooned with antibiotics, to help her wounds heal in the brackish water.

The day the whales were on the move back toward the sea, I got up early to retrieve my phone before I went to work. I also had a secret agenda.

I had seen the dead coyote on the side of Highway 4 and decided I wanted to bring it home. I had started digging a hole alongside the fence in my backyard, a ready grave for the cat when the time came. I kept it covered with an overturned galvanized tub. I planned to bury the coyote there.

That morning I stopped at Safeway to get black plastic trash bags. I continued planning how I would pick up the creature that I had claimed as my Miwok Spirit Trickster. I felt fear and exhilaration as I imagined how I would slide the bag over the coyote. I knew the body couldn't be that heavy. Then I'd hoist it into my trunk as the cars rushed by. I felt like a hit man planning how to dispose of the evidence.

Then, on the car radio I heard that the whales were swimming from the Benicia Bridge down toward the Carquinez Bridge, just by our house.

I continued rolling down Highway 4 and then I spotted the shape of the coyote road kill on the side of the road. I pulled the car over near the curled-up furry mound. I tried to pull the black plastic over the *Canis latrans*, but I realized I couldn't do it without touching the body. I had to lift the coyote's shoulder so it would slip inside the bag. My hand was smeared with blood and I was heady with the smells of musk, danger, and animal decomps. The smells thrilled me and scared me.

Then I lifted the double black plastic bag into my trunk and drove to work. The smell was on me; the blood and the smell were on my steering wheel and on my gearshift. I had to wash my hands before I went up to the lab. I was lucky a single bathroom was available on the first floor just inside the door. My heart was pounding hard. I stopped there and scrubbed my hands and arms with soap, and wiped the blood off my shoes.

I went upstairs hoping I wouldn't be discovered by the smell, and hoping no one would notice the death smell coming from the trunk of my car. To my advantage, the lab downstairs was working with animals that day and they were producing smells of their own.

I tried to stop thinking about the coyote in the trunk of my car. I tried to concentrate on my work, but my mind was pounding with the fear of being discovered.

The movement of the whales caused great excitement, so I called Kennan and found he was at the viewing platform just upriver from C & H Sugar. He had seen the whales pass by upstream from the road to Port Costa and they were coming down fast. The whale sighting was a good cover story. I told my work mates that I was going to go see the whales, but my real intention was to bury the coyote in my backyard.

I was in a hurry because I did want to see the whales, but this desire was overshadowed by the primal need to get rid of the body. I rushed home. When I got there, no one was home. Kennan was still upstream watching the mother whale and her calf elude the media and the Coast Guard.

I hauled the double plastic bag up the backyard stairs and uncovered the hole. I could see that the hole was too small and too shallow, so I worked up a sweat, digging it out more. When the hole was big enough, I poured the limp fur and bones in the hole.

The wild dog looked like it was sleeping in the earth, curled up in a cozy ball, peaceful. I began to cover it with dirt, but just then, Kennan called up from below. Excited about the movement of the whales, he was already up on the deck with binoculars, scanning the Carquinez Straits. I shoveled and patted the soil firm, wadded up the black plastic bags, and shoved them down in the outside trash bin. This turned out to be the smoking gun, the reeking bags. The next day, I turned my eyes down when Kennan admonished me,

"I'm trying not to ask too many questions, but the garbage smells like a dead animal. Whatever you put in there, don't do it again."

I didn't confess. I was pretty sure the trouble I would face for bringing home a dead coyote would be worse than the trouble I faced for bringing home a live puppy.

Coyote runs through the Miwok Legends. Sometimes Creator,

sometimes Trickster, he plays the Cosmic joke on the humans. The Miwok Indians tell a story of creation in which Coyote sends a duck to dive to the bottom of the water and come up with some earth. Coyote takes the earth and mixes it with Chanit seeds and water. The mixture swells and "the earth was there." The Diver Coyote created the earth and land from the endless water. The Coast Miwok tell a story of the afterlife, they say the dead jumped into the ocean at Point Reyes and followed something like a string leading west beyond the breaker waves that took them to the setting sun. There they remained with Coyote in an afterworld "ute-yomigo" or "ute-yomi," meaning "dead home." [†]

In the days that followed, I learned it is true that we live in a dog-eat-dog world. I tried to keep the grave covered, but it was shallow, and my pet dogs exhumed part of the wild one. On the patio out back, I found an upper jawbone with teeth and I kept it, safe out of the jaw's reach of the coyote's domestic canine brethren. That coyote maxilla and teeth have become a link and a relic to the Coast Miwok Spirit buried in my home earth.

[†] Kroeber, Alfred L. 1907. "Indian Myths of South Central California" University of California Publications in American Archaeology and Ethnology 4:203. Berkeley. Southern Sierra Miwok myths: Earth Diver, p. 203.

CHAPTER 6

BEAUTY RANCH

Jack London's life was short, but eventful. In spite of suffering from alcoholism, he traveled worldwide, worked as a war journalist, produced an acclaimed body of literary works, and shared a profound bond with his third wife, Charmian Kittredge London. Jack and Charmian London are buried together under a boulder on the grounds of Beauty Ranch near the town of Glen Ellen in Sonoma County, California.

And two pioneer children, David and Lily Greenlaw are buried in a forlorn patch of brush on a hill on the property. A picket fence encloses their grave markers. Jack had once told Charmian, "I wouldn't mind if you laid my ashes on the knoll where the Greenlaw children are buried. And roll over me a red boulder from the ruins of the Big House."

Jack London's story is one of meteoric rise and cataclysmic ruin. Again and again, he soared and plunged until his body and soul wore out, and he succumbed. At the apex of Jack London's life, he found Charmian to be his perfect match. They fenced and sailed the seas, and she typed his manuscripts. Together they designed and built the Wolf House.

Just as the Big House of their dreams was completed, Wolf House burned to stone-hearth ruins, in a spontaneous flash of destruction, the same way Jack London burned out his life.

The circumstances of Jack's death are debated. London biographer Richard O'Connor wrote:

Charmian, according to a later statement by Dr. Thompson, argued that his death must be attributed to natural causes. Whether the attending physicians were swayed by her pleas or not, they joined in concealing the cause of death; it remained a secret, so far as the public was concerned, until 1938, when Irving Stone's Sailor on Horseback was published. "When Dr. Porter signed Jack's death certificate, he stated that the cause of death was 'uremia following renal colic with chronic interstitial nephritis as a contributing cause.' ...Later that night the newsboys in Oakland, outside low-life hangouts where he had freely spent his time, money, and health, shouted the news that John Barleycorn had finally claimed a favorite son."

Jack London died in 1916 when he was only forty years old. But the steady, faithful, bright and adventurous Charmian remained on Beauty Ranch. She built the House of Happy Walls and lived there among the objects and memories she and Jack had collected from their travels. In 1955, Charmian Kittredge London died at the age of 84 and was interred beside Jack under the same boulder on the knoll.

Dusty came along with me the day I went to Beauty Ranch to dig dirt from under the London's boulder. I had already collected Ina Coolbrith from Mountain View cemetery in Oakland and I brought along a paper sack containing some of Ina's grave dirt with me to Glen Ellen.

I walked down the path from the parking lot past the House of Happy Walls into the woods. Signs posted at the trailhead warned against poison oak and rattlesnakes. Alongside the path, I saw manzanitas, their paper-thin epidermis peeled off to reveal blood-red bark. Blackberry bushes tempted me with their purple-black fruit.

I began picking the berries and popping them into my mouth one after the other. I reached into the bramble just a bit farther to harvest the berries. The branches caught my sleeves; the thorns scratched my arms and pricked my skin. I licked my red-stained fingers and smacked my red-stained lips.

Before long, I had to tear myself away, because no sooner had I popped a half sour blackberry in my mouth than I found a dangling trove of black fruit that promised to be sweet.

Along the path, I heard the rustle of lizards startled during their sun bathing. I was happy to see bees pollinating flowers, for I remembered the bee population was in trouble in Northern California.

Soon, the path opened to the ruins of the Wolf House. I took pictures of the ruins from all sides against the backdrop of the redwoods. The setting seemed holy, like the Mayan ruins in the rainforest of Belize.

On the small landing at the top of the stone steps I found a desiccated bird, its bones and feathers, beak and feet intact. I tucked the little dead bird in a paper bag and put it in my backpack.

A picket fence encloses the gravesite, with a sign that reads Jack London's Grave. I bruised my 44-year-old ass climbing the fence, while Dusty sat outside the fence as a sentry guard.

I bought and paid for Jack and Charmian's intermingled grave dirt with silver dimes, and I poured Ancient Age spirits into shot glasses that overflowed in the ground. Then I mixed some of Ina's dirt in the London's grave as a posthumous reunion of the writer and his literary mother.

Ina wrote this poem:

Beside the Dead

It must be sweet, O thou, my dead, to lie

With hands that folded are from every task,

Sealed with the seal of the great mystery, -

The lips that nothing answer, nothing ask;

The life-long struggle ended; ended quite

The weariness of patience and of pain;

And the eyes closed to open not again

On desolate dawn or dreariness of night.

It must be sweet to slumber and forget-

To have the poor tired heart so still, at last:

Done with all yearning, done with all regret;

Doubt, fear, hope, sorrow, all for ever past—

Past all the hours, or slow of wing or fleet-

It must be sweet, it must be very sweet!

July 14, 1993, Bastille Day was the day my husband Kennan gave up drinking. Up until that day, he had been a longtime drinking man and had an almost daily habit of sliding into a stupor, passing out and snoring.

I can't say it didn't bother me, his drinking was messy and inconvenient, but drinking was expected behavior for musicians who played bar gigs and were rewarded with free booze and a few bucks from the tip jar.

The night of July 13, 1993, I got a phone call from the El Cerrito police saying they had Kennan in custody; there had been an accident and he had been arrested for drunk driving. They told me no other cars were involved and no one was hurt. I had to pick him up at the station, so I scooped up baby Jack, and we went to get Kennan. I remember the looks of tragic sympathy on the faces of the cops when I came in with a little kid on my hip.

We did what we needed to do, signed the necessary papers, and Kennan was released to me. That night Kennan cried in my arms. The next day I said to him, "You can do whatever you want in response to this accident, as far as drinking or quitting. It is completely your choice. I will make my decision based on what you decide."

Kennan has not had a drink since that night. That was 1993, and in hindsight, the accident and arrest were among the best things that ever happened to us. July 14, Bastille Day, 1993, was a crossroads moment in my life. Fuck John Barleycorn, he doesn't have any power here.

I first met Kennan at his parent's house when I was 17. His sister Kari was my high school friend and it was my turn to sleep over at her house. That night Kennan came in late with a friend. We all laughed and talked, then Kari went to bed and the friend left. Kennan and I were alone that night in 1979. We kissed for a while, nothing more. I developed a crush that went unrequited for five years.

The Shaw family house was on a busy street in Walnut Creek. Whenever I drove by, I checked to see who was inside. I always hoped to see Kennan. Sometimes I saw his parents, Lora and Earl. It was easy to see who was in the kitchen when the light was on and it was dark outside.

Five years passed and in 1984, I was invited to go to Santa Cruz with Kari, Kennan and a cousin from Oklahoma. We met up at Kari's apartment. When I walked in, Kennan's eyebrows went up and his mouth hung open. This is the way I tell the story. If he wants to tell a different story, he can write his own. Anyway, I could tell Kennan was interested in me.

On the way to Santa Cruz, we were crowded in the back seat of the car so my arm touched his. He was quiet, but an electric charge ran through the fibers of our clothes where we touched.

When we got to the Boardwalk at Santa Cruz, we hung out as a group, riding rides and eating corn dogs. The Giant Dipper rollercoaster and the bumper cars were cool, but my favorite ride was the Merry-go-

Round. The riders on the outside animals can pull a brass ring every time around and try to throw the ring in the Clown's mouth. If you hit it, a bell rings and a buzzer sounds.

After a while, Kennan separated me from the herd by getting me to go on the Sky Lift where our feet dangled above the park. I found out later that Kennan was afraid of heights. During that ride, he was determined not to look down, so he focused on me by asking me questions.

"Where are you working now?"

"I just started at Chevron Chemical where my Dad works. My job is analyzing crops for pesticide residues. How about you?"

"I work in my parents business, Brekas Type and Graphics, in Berkeley. The whole family works there."

The small talk served as a distraction until our feet landed on terra firma as we jumped off the Sky Lift.

But the Cave Train was the place we fell in love. I grabbed Kennan's leg, startled by the prehistoric cartoon caveman who popped out from behind a rock, and the rest is history.

Kennan and I lived together in Martinez, then Albany, Berkeley, and El Cerrito, all in California. After Jack was born, we bought the house in Crockett.

In about 1990, Kennan got back into playing bass. I remember gigs with the Rubbles on weeknights at the Hotel Utah in San Francisco or at Merchants in the produce district of Oakland, a weird place beeping with nocturnal activity. Forklifts blew their backup horns as they moved pallets of lettuce. The lights in the warehouse awnings made the night seem like day.

Kennan rehearsed on Wednesday nights with the Random Dudes, a band made up of good friends, headed up by Eric Delore, singer-songwriter.

Some years later, Kennan went fretless. The blues gigs and jam nights rolled into days, months and years. I can't remember the names of all the bands he's played with. Danny Click took Kennan to festival tour dates in Fiji, New Zealand and Lugano, Switzerland.

In 2007, Kennan got a gig as bass player for John Lee Hooker Jr. John Junior was the oldest son of the legendary John Lee Hooker. For about a year, Kennan traveled with Junior's band in what he now calls the Short White Bus of the Blues.

John Junior had done hard time and still conducted some aspects of his business like prison transactions. His young guitarist was a talent, a barely-functional alcoholic, a damaged guy. The drummer was missing some teeth, didn't have a solid home, but had a talent for acquiring free weed at all the stops along the road of life. The keyboard player was another pothead and an insufferable weirdo. They were all damaged. Kennan was the only one who had something to go home to.

After a year of driving the Short White Bus of the Blues like a maniac and almost dying in a snowstorm like the Donner party, Kennan came home and left the John Lee Hooker Jr. Band to find a new bass player. For a rambling man, Kennan turned out to be a real homebody.

Now, in 2010, Kennan plays bass for Candye Kane. He's on the road a lot.

—

The kids are big now, coming of age. Jack is 18 and Carolyn is 15 years old. When Jack walks away from me, the way he moves reminds me of my dad, Paul. But Jack is a lot like me. A cord connects my son's psyche to mine. Kennan accuses Jack and me of having the same brain, the same mind.

Carolyn's her own person and often the voice of reason when ramshackle, haphazard ideas pop into my head. Sometimes I call her my Dream Pooper. My job is to spin wild ideas and her job is to question them.

"I think we should open an ice cream parlor in Crockett and I'll have a horse and I'll tie it up outside to a hitching post in front of the store."

Then Carolyn performs her valuable dream-pooping function.

"First of all, where are we going to keep a horse? Second, how are we going to pay for the rent of the ice cream parlor? Plus, it will cost a lot to get that set up and I doubt if we'll make that much money. Besides, who's gonna work there?"

"Fine. Just poop on my dreams."

Carolyn rolls her eyes, "I'm just saying."

My daughter is a strong young woman, poised, sarcastic, confident and grown up, but there are times when she still wants to be taken care of.

"Mom, can you make me some French Toast?"

"The usual?"

She smiles and nods. When it's ready, I bring her French Toast, all cut up, with butter and brown sugar and powdered sugar.

"I love you, Mommy."

CHAPTER 7

WATERSHED

My parents, Paul and Theresa called 1995 a watershed year for the Lipton family. In 1995, Carolyn was born, and my sister Debbie made her reappearance. That year, my parents bought a house in Berkeley and made the move back to Northern California. My brother Tom got married, a week before Kennan and I, just so he could be first.

Carolyn's birth was the first big event of 1995.

Late January, 1995 I called my parents to come to Crockett from their place in La Habra; I insisted that our second baby was on the way. My parents showed up and sat in my house, staring at me on the couch, checking their watches and pacing, awaiting the arrival of the latest grandchild. Carolyn was born on February 3, 1995.

Carolyn has always been fearless and stubborn. She was a two month old bundle when the family attended the Seder at Fay Goleman's house in Stockton. Carolyn was just seven months old when Kennan and I got married on the front porch of our house in Crockett. My Aunt Ann held her most of the day inside the house while the festivities rolled on outside. As a consequence, we have no video of Carolyn at the wedding and she is still mad about it.

Before Carolyn was two years old, she decided that she wanted to run as fast as she could into the Pacific Ocean, so she did, again and again. Kennan had to chase her over and over. Nothing we told her would convince her invincible mind that it was not a good idea to run into the ocean before you have learned to swim.

One day I told her, "Stop picking your nose."

"I'm not picking it. I'm just getting the hard stuff out."

When Carolyn was in the middle of kindergarten, maybe five and a half years old, we attended a cousin's wedding in Puerto Vallarta. Fancy water slides hung over the pool at the resort, and both kids went down them with no fear. The hotel had supervised activities for the kids. So, while eight-year-old Jack was on the beach, playing with the younger kids, teaching them and coaching them, Carolyn was on the surfboard in the pool with the twenty-something yoo-hoos, hitting the volleyball around and shooting orange juice while the other players shot tequila.

One day, when Carolyn was small, we went to Mr. Mopp's toy store in Berkeley. She became fixated on a play kitchen set. Carolyn was so intent and so focused she ignored our commands and pleas and cajoles to pull her away. No matter what we said, she continued cooking, stirring the toy pots with a fury. Carolyn ignored us with such profound concentration, I believe for a few moments that day we ceased to exist.

When I was a kid in Berkeley, I'd walk up to Mr. Mopp's with my
one dollar allowance and I'd buy a paperback book. Sometimes I'd get a
troll with bright-colored hair. Other times I'd buy a chunk of Mexican
chocolate from the shop near the intersection of Virginia and Grove Street,
or a frozen slush from the Rose and Grove Market.

The crossroads at Virginia and McGee in Berkeley was the epicenter
of my childhood happenings. All the neighborhood kids played at Totland
Park. I was so little I had to climb up on the base of the drinking fountain
and stand on my toes to get a drink. A small school building stood there
and we would all dig the putty out from around the metal window frames,
but my brother was the one who got caught.

I remember swinging at Totland with my first true love, a boy the
age of four. Our legs pumped into the sky until our feet touched outer
space together. Then we jumped off and landed in the sand.

I remember working hard in the Boat Yard, with the sandpaper
block my dad had fixed for me, sanding Chuck's boat, the wooden boat he
was building to sail to Tahiti. We called him Chucky-Wucky-Kentucky-
Fried-Chicken and he was my second true love. I planned to marry
him some day. Friends gathered in the boatyard for food and folk songs.
My mom strummed her acoustic guitar and sang, "The Fox Went Out
on a Chilly Night." I was bundled by the fire, anticipating my favorite
part of the song: "and the little ones chewed on the Bones-O, Bones-O,
Bones-O. They'd never had such a supper in their life and the little ones
chewed on the Bones-O".

We hung out with commercial fishermen and climbed to the rafters of the cannery in Monterey. Even our shaggy dog, Cholly, climbed a ladder to get to the top of the defunct cannery, where we had to balance on the bare floor joists to get around.

On early morning low tides, our family and friends would travel to Tomales Bay for clamming. My Mom could dig more clams than anyone. She tossed them in the bucket and cooked them right on the beach, and then we devoured them with garlic butter and sourdough bread.

The 1960's were in full force and Vietnam was everywhere. I saw peace protests and soldiers in camouflage with guns, riding in army trucks on the streets of Berkeley. My dad carried me on his shoulders as we marched to People's Park that day.

And I knew that the war was wrong, but Vietnam had always been there. Dylan, Baez, and Guthrie sang the protest songs about the war, and draft dodgers, and conscientious objectors. Blowing in the wind, with God on our side and you can get anything you want, at Alice's Restaurant.

Out Now was everywhere, on buttons and stickers, painted on walls alongside peace-sign graffiti. Psychedelic Pop Art posters hung on the wall, LOVE in block letters by Robert Indiana. I remember a poster of a crooked daisy that said: WAR is not healthy for children or other living things.

We collected buttons and the colored thumbtacks from telephone poles where bills were posted that talked about revolution and peace on the same, stapled paper. The small sign on my friend Harriet's bulletin board said, "Why do we kill people, who have killed people, to show people that killing is wrong?"

Every one in the world hated Nixon as far as I could tell. As far as my nine-year-old eyes could see, the messages on Volkswagens and Volvos, Karman Ghias and house signs, the paper bills posted on poles and boards, all made me certain that McGovern would win in 1972.

Then I woke up. I realized Berkeley was not the center of the Universe. All the things I learned in Black Studies about Dr. King and Malcolm X and Civil Rights were not matters settled in the distant past; these struggles were happening all around me.

By age 10, I understood it all.

When I was 11 and my brother Tom was 12-and-a-half, we set off from Antioch, California to Mexico with my mother's older brother, Uncle Ernie Pigati. Ernie and his wife Irene invited us to visit them in the big house called Casa Irene. They'd retired to Mexico and built two houses on the hill above Puerto Vallarta, the sleepy resort that Elizabeth Taylor and Richard Burton had made famous.

The drive took four days. The vehicle was an International Harvester Scout, the proto-SUV. Our payload: half a dozen rifles hidden under the floorboards of the truck, and two kennels with yelping, pooping puppies. Both the dogs and the guns would be used for hunting. Ernie led hunting expeditions in the jungle rain forests near P.V. The year was 1974.

We set off from Antioch down through Arizona and entered

Mexico through the border crossing at Nogales. Uncle Ernie did all the driving. My traveling companions were my brother Tom, a 13-year-old kid named Jeff and the puppies. I was the only girl. We took turns washing out the dog kennels and I kept track of mileage and expenses in my ledger.

At checkpoints along the way, the Mexican Federales poked around the back of the Scout, shining their flashlights and asking questions. Uncle Ernie gave them a tip and I recorded these expenses in my ledger along with food, gas and lodging.

When we got to Puerto Vallarta, we were treated like dirty, sun-burned, mosquito-bitten kings. I learned the hard way that there's a reason to close the shutters at night. One night my brother made me believe he put a scorpion in my bed. We shopped in the market and bought parrots and switchblades. We rode in taxis and slid down waterfalls in the river. After a month of Lord-of-the-Flies hedonistic bliss, we flew back to San Diego where our parents picked us up and took us home.

Tom and I had smuggled a couple of switchblades home and Dad confiscated them. He reimbursed us for the cost of our contraband, so we had no monetary claims on the switchblades.

In 1975, my family moved to Concord, to a house on Cuneo Drive. Cuneo Drive was a private, partially-paved road, with potholes and ditches that ran along both sides, but no sidewalks. I remember being surprised by the lack of sidewalks. Berkeley was all sidewalks.

Houses ran along one side of Cuneo Drive. On the other side was open property owned by Mr. Cuneo, the elder, who was already in his nineties when we moved there. Mr. Cuneo, the younger was in his seventies. Their property was scattered with rusted out farm equipment, storage tanks, sheds and out-buildings. The house where the old men lived was on a dirt road. Old Mr. Cuneo still hoed his garden by hand. One year, I think, the younger Mr. Cuneo borrowed our roto-tiller to turn the soil for planting. Mr. Cuneo the younger, played the accordion and wore flannel shirts, suspenders and work boots.

Tom was about 13 when he befriended Mr. Cuneo the elder and spent time in his workshop learning to work with tools. The Liptons are pursuers of useful knowledge.

Our house on Cuneo Drive was a single floor ranch-style that sat on ½ acre. My mother kept chickens and goats. She grew vegetables, potatoes and squash in her garden and we ate brown eggs and drank goat's milk. One year we had pigs. My mom fed the pigs and massaged them with her feet. She loved them.

Week in and week out, my dad dug ditches to bury the pig shit. He hated them.

My Grandpa Louis Pigati had experience with pig slaughtering and butchering, so he came to help my dad and my uncle David kill the pigs. Grandma Pigati stayed in the house with my mom and Tom and me. I remember hearing the gunshots and some yelling from the backyard.

We stayed out of the way while the grownups dressed the hogs and butchered the meat. I remember buckets of pig blood on the bottom shelf of the refrigerator in the garage. We were saving it to make blood sausage.

Keeping animals means you have to learn to deal with them dying.

Behind the chicken shed in the backyard of our house on Cuneo drive was a deep square hole we called the pit. I never looked under the plywood lid that covered the hole, but I knew that was the place to put dead things because they would decompose there at a rapid rate.

One time when we were in the backyard, my brother handed me his BB gun. I held it in a loose grip aimed downward, point blank at Tom's stomach, and somehow, I squeezed the trigger. Bam! Tom doubled over, held his stomach and yelled. I started screaming because I thought I'd killed my brother. Tom straightened up and yelled at me to shut up, because he didn't want Mom to find out he had handed me his BB gun. He had a bad bruise where I shot him, but the skin was not broken.

When we were older, Tom had moved out, but I was still living at home, I remember a green backpack I had that I thought was cool. It was a genuine, well-made, tough, durable piece of camping and hiking gear. I never said my brother could use it, but Tom's attitude was, well, if I wasn't using it, he might as well use it to haul his stuff to and from work. At that time Tom had a job in San Francisco working for Thrasher magazine, designing or building go-carts. On workdays, Tom rode BART to work from the Concord BART station to San Francisco.

One morning, Tom needed both hands free to purchase a BART ticket, so he held the green backpack between his legs while he fed the dollar bill into the machine. The backpack slipped out and fell to the ground.

"Bam!"

People started looking all around, "What was that? What was that?"
Tom did the same.

"What was that?" he said.

After a few moments of confusion, the commuters shrugged off the sound and went on their way, into the station and up to the platform to wait for a train.

Tom did the same. He went to work with a .22 slug lodged in his thigh, worked for eight hours and took BART home. The homemade zip-gun he was carrying in my backpack had gone off when he dropped it on the ground. Not wanting to call attention to the source of the gunshot, Tom continued as if nothing had happened.

When he got home that night, his girlfriend Sargamo tried to get Tom to go to the Emergency Room, but Tom knew the police would be called in for any gunshot wound. Tom tried to deal with it at home, but fever set in. He knew he'd have to go to the hospital, so he crafted his story and went to Emergency.

After a round of antibiotics and an examination of the wound, the doctors decided to leave the bullet in. The trauma of cutting through all the thigh muscle to get it out would be worse than leaving it alone. The cops believed the story my brother told about the accidental discharge of the registered .22 caliber gun he had at home.

Tom still has that slug in his thigh. The bullet hole ruined my green backpack.

CHAPTER 8

FALLING TREES

—◄—

On Lakeville Road in Sonoma County, California, a stand of ancient towering Eucalyptus trees line the roadway at intervals for a few miles. These trees are tall and old, and have stood for one hundred years or more, a full lifespan for a Eucalyptus. Now, some of the branches and limbs are beginning to fall. There are signs along Lakeville Road that read, "Falling Trees" to warn passersby of the danger. And there are homemade signs that read: "Save the Lakeville Trees. Sign up at Ernie's Tin Bar."

Even to the occasional traveler on this road, it is obvious that people are engaged in a controversy and a conversation about whether the "Falling Trees" should be cut down or allowed to stand.

My mom would say, "They're an invasive species, not native to California, and they present a fire hazard."

My dad would say, "I'm glad to hear someone is interested in saving the Eucalyptus trees."

I drove with my mentor, Kate along Lakeville Road on the way to Forestville, California. Kate is a towering intellect with encyclopedic knowledge, and a vast academic, personal and life experience. She has a PhD in Microbiology and waxes poetic about meiosis, nitrogen fixation and orthnithology. During that drive we talked about crows. The conversation started when I posed this question.

"When I was a kid in Berkeley, I never saw a crow. Now I see them everywhere. Do you have any idea why that is?"

As expected, Kate provided answers, "Well, crows are much more successful these days in urban environments than they are around farms. Think about it. The way agriculture is now in the rural areas, they'd have to fly miles to get the range of foods that they need, but it's easy for crows in the cities. Crows are taking over the cities. Some cities have had to spend a significant part of their budgets to get the crows out."

"So scarecrows don't work?"

"I don't think scarecrows ever worked. Crows are very intelligent and social. The roosting area is a central place where multigenerational tribes band together. As a matter of fact, in Seattle, in Pioneer Square, there are some lovely trees and wonderful shaded sitting areas, but for a while, when the crow population was thick, humans would get dive-bombed, bombarded and pooped on by the hundreds and hundreds of crows that had taken up residence in the trees.

"The first thing the city tried, to get rid of them, was to put huge black plastic bags over the trees," Kate continued. "The birds were flummoxed at first, until they realized they could tear through the bags and go back to their roosts.

"The second attempt to get rid of the crows involved loud booming noises and twirly, shiny, spinning disks. Those methods didn't work, either. The crows didn't mind any of this, but the booms were startling the humans, so that effort was abandoned.

"Then they tried to remove food sources from the area and imposed very strict garbage disposal ordinances and installed special crow-proof garbage cans around Pioneer Square."

"Did that work?"

"Nope. The crows just flew to other neighborhoods for food and came back to the Pioneer Square trees to roost and build nests."

"Did they ever get them out?"

"Yeah, what finally worked was poking tiny holes in their eggs."

"What did that do?"

"The crows continued to incubate them, but they couldn't hatch. And as long as they're incubating eggs they won't breed."

"Okay, so the population goes down slowly. That seems kind of cruel."

"Yeah, but what are you going to do? Nothing else worked."

"Man, that's a lot of work, climbing up in the trees and sticking pins in the crow's eggs."

"It was hugely labor-intensive."

Kate continued to tell stories about crows and I listened with interest as we rolled past Petaluma.

"Crows are amazing imitators," Kate explained. "I was watching a crow one time, and he was watching a seagull. The seagull was skimming food off of the surface of the water. Seagulls have webbed feet and they can swim, but crows do not have webbed feet and they can't swim. But that crow watched the seagull do it over and over. I watched the crow do his practice flight, imitating the way the seagull had come in. After watching and practicing, the crow was able to do it, too. That would be like you or me watching an ice skater do a triple Lutz and then just going out on the ice and doing it."

"I could probably pull off a triple Klutz."

"Yeah, probably."

"I also read that young crows will do what's called anting."

"Anting? What is that?"

"They'll find an ant's nest and they'll puff out their chest feathers until their skin is exposed and they'll wriggle down onto the ants nest and get high as the red ants bite them and the venom gets in their blood."

"Sounds just like teenagers and Jack Daniels."

"Yeah. Exactly."

The Lipton Family is a mob of autodidacts. My dad, Paul, who is probably a genius, dropped out of college and worked his whole career as an analytical chemist doing complex instrumental analysis. He learned what he needed to learn and synthesized his knowledge and experience into a highly regarded professional career. His *Curriculum Vitae* reads like that of a normal PhD scientist, except that it is uncluttered by any university degrees.

My organic mother, Theresa, is a self-taught expert in plants and horticulture, and an accomplished ceramic craftsperson. She has raised goats, chickens and pigs. She taught ceramics when my parents had a small shop called Earth 'n Wares in Berkeley. I remember the store at the corner of Ashby Avenue and Adeline Street.

My brother is a metal worker recently employed by Lawrence Berkeley Laboratories to work on advanced fission projects. He has also published a book. No degree.

My husband, Kennan plays bass guitar and has worked with a range of musicians and groups. He has toured the world with various acts, in between raising our two kids. He did all this while I worked for local Bay Area pharmaceutical and biotechnology companies.

I learned on the job, gaining the knowledge I needed through experience and self-study. During my career, working in R&D-intensive scientific industries that are regulated by federal government agencies, I have met a lot of PhDs. A few have become my close friends and we have shared confidences with one another.

In the course of my life experience, two PhD mentors have punched me in the gut and then turned their backs on me. The blows knocked the wind out of me and left me doubled over. I have rationalized that getting a PhD requires an obsessive-compulsive, tenacious, territorial personality. But my heart still feels like a crumpled paper when I remember. The first betrayal was spiritual.

I thought that my relationship with a PhD named Thomas had deep roots in our shared exploration of dream symbols and archetypal constellations. We worked together for many years and I trusted him as my wise old man archetype. I revered him as a prophet in the body of a nerdy, greasy-haired, PhD chemist. The year I turned thirty, Thomas turned fifty. He'd had a nervous breakdown a few years earlier and was working at making sense of life from a Jungian perspective.

Every morning for years, I listened to his strange dreams and his interpretations. We talked about Carl Gustav Jung, active imagination, synchronicity, and anima and animus projections.

Thomas had been raised Catholic in Oakland, California. He attended Bishop O'Dowd Catholic High school. His wife, also a PhD, worked for IBM. They had a daughter. The family lived in Fremont and their home was decorated Danish Modern.

Thomas led me to one of my most cherished heirlooms. My dead ancestors have communicated with me through letters left behind, a locket hidden in an old leather case, opera glasses, and this time through a poem by Leonard Cohen.

Thomas kept a book of Leonard Cohen poems at his desk and once in a while he would read them aloud with his lispy voice. One morning, Thomas finished reading and handed me the book with his bright eyes and boyish grin,

"Now, you read me one," he said.

I opened the book at random and began to read the poem on the page where I happened to land. The poem was called Heirloom.

The torture scene developed under a glass bell,

such as might protect an expensive clock.

I almost expected a chime to sound as the tongs were applied

and the body jerked and fainted calm.

All the people were tiny and rosy-cheeked

and if I could have heard a cry of triumph or pain,

it would have been tiny as the mouth that made it,

or one single note of a music box.

The drama bell was mounted.

Like a giant baroque pearl

on a wedding ring or brooch or locket.

I know you feel naked little darling,

I know you hate living in the country

and can't wait until the shiny magazines,

come every week and every month.

Look through your grandmother's house again.

There is an heirloom somewhere.

I finished reading aloud, hung up on the last two lines of the poem. Thomas looked up with a slight start. I was puzzled.

"There's a message there for you."

"What is it?" I said, as he waited for me to figure it out myself.

"The last two lines. Don't you have the boxes of papers from your grandmother?" Thomas prompted me.

"Yes." I read the two small lines again, "Look through your

grandmother's house again. There's an heirloom somewhere."

I paused as the words sunk into my brain.

I looked up from the book to face my smiling prophet with his thick glasses and greasy, stringy hair. The meaning was so clear, cloaked in its simplicity. If Thomas had not pressed it toward me, I would have missed the obvious.

"There's something in there you are supposed to find."

That evening, I unpacked the cardboard boxes again and this time I found the folder that contained my Grandma Mildred's writings.

It was a meaningful coincidence, synchronicity. I made the connection. When I saw what the poem signified, I stretched my mind. The meaning touched down like a moth landing on a twig. My grandmother's heirloom found me, posthumously.

I held the thin folder in my hands. "Mom's Writings" was pencil scratched on the outside in my father's handwriting. I opened the folder and claimed my inheritance.

Years later came the betrayal. I didn't think it was possible for such a complete and irrevocable fissure to form between two human beings after sharing a profound connection. In my life, it has only happened with two humans, both PhDs.

Roman Catholics the world over are connected because of shared ritual and numinous experience. It's impossible for me to participate in this connection, because I was and am an unbaptized pagan baby who could never understand. Still, I was confident that because of all the metaphysical and philosophical discussions I had had with Thomas, I would be welcome. He had led me to a precious heirloom and guided me to listen to the voices of my ancestors. Since I had listened to his meditations and dreams for years, I felt sure he would include me when he circled back to the spiritual experience of his youth.

Blake Garden is perched in the hills above Berkeley. It is a botanical garden, open to the public. On the grounds of Blake Garden sits a fancy house that is the official residence of the President of the Regents of the University of California. It is a magnificent house with a panoramic view wrapping from Oakland to the South, beyond Richmond to the North, and to the City across the Bay Bridge to the West.

Surrounding the house are formal Italian gardens and roses. In a ravine, a stand of California Redwoods towers. Along the property line to the North, a solid wooden slat fence separates Blake Garden from a cloistered Carmelite Convent. I have often tried to find cracks in the fence, or open knotholes so I could peek at what the nuns were doing on the other side.

A tiny Catholic Church also stands on the front of the property, a sanctuary where the Priest holds Mass for the nuns. The altar is facing inward for the cloistered sisters. Visitors to the church watch from behind as the nuns take communion.

Thomas planned a mini-pilgrimage to the tiny church.

I was not included.

It wasn't only because Thomas excluded me from this adventure that I was crushed; the betrayal went much deeper.

At this time, a young woman worked with us named Chelsea. She was from Wyoming and had a Jackson Hole in her soul the size of Cheyenne. In my estimation, Chelsea was one of the most shallow, self-centered, privileged people I had ever known. She reeked with her smug sense of entitlement.

However, Chelsea had been raised Catholic.

I don't think Chelsea cared enough about Thomas to go along on the expedition. I don't think she really cared much about anyone. But she had been was baptized Catholic, and that was what mattered.

I was the only person from work who really wanted to go along with Thomas, to participate in his numinous quest. Thomas and I had talked about spiritual exploration for so long. I had listened. He was my prophet and he turned his back on me. I have not forgiven him.

Kate also turned her back on me. I betrayed her when I offered a job to her Microbiology Technician, Wendy. And I killed the staghorn fern Kate left in my care. Both of these epiphytic creatures were important to Kate. She nurtured them and I took them away from her. From the day Wendy accepted my job offer, I was Anathema to Kate. She never asked me to return the staghorn fern.

I have a heart-shaped box made out of cinnamon wood that Kate gave me. Kate taught me about recombinant DNA technology and crows. The cinnamon box fits in my hand. I love to remove the lid and smell the cinnamon inside. Kate also gave me a handcrafted silver necklace that I still wear. These small things are all I have left of Kate. Everything else is gone.

I read an excerpt from a short paper I found among the writings by my grandmother Mildred in the heirloom folder:

> *The intellectual snobs admit no universality of human wants and needs and yearnings. They feel themselves to be elevated to a rare atmosphere, which only they can breathe, having acquired some extraordinary physical appendage, some exquisitely refined gill, with the acquisition of a degree in fine arts. They deliberately build a barrier which none can pass unless he is first subjected to a physical examination which must reveal the presence of the gill. If the gill proves to be degree of M.A. or more unusual blue gill of Ph.D, the owners are given positions in rarer and rarest atmosphere, and so men stratify themselves, and there is no communication between them and those who breathe the heavy air of intellectual yearnings.*

That's me. I breathe the heavy air with you, Grandma.

Mildred Formento ca. 1934.

Morris Lipstein, 1932, upon graduation from Medical School.

Left photo: Morrie and Mil ca. 1942.

Below: Mil on the left with a classmate, Willard Hospital, Chicago, 1930s.

Morrie overseas during WWII.

Mil in traditional Sioux dress in Rosebud, SD, ca. 1939.

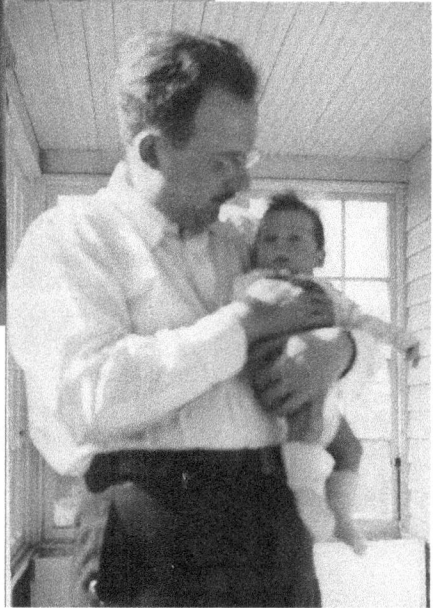

Morrie with Paul Lipton (my Dad) in Rosebud, SD, 1939.

*Mil and little Paul, bundled up for South Dakota winter,
ca. 1940*

CHAPTER 9

DR. AND MRS. M.L. LIPTON

———

After she suffered her massive stroke, my Grandmother Mildred Lipton could no longer speak. I remember Grandma's paralyzed right hand resting in her lap, and her sweet crooked smile. The right side of her face was slack, but both eyes glistened with sharp delight, and sometimes disdain.

Grandma Lipton was born in Chicago, Illinois in 1911, to Italian immigrants. Her parents were Paul Formento and Isabella Del Re. The ship manifest reveals that neither Paul nor Isabella could read or write much, but they were determined to make a life in Chicago. My grandma Mil was the second of four children, Rose was the oldest, and then Mil, then Violet; Michael was the youngest.

My grandmother's baptismal certificate says Carmella Formento, but she was a self-determining woman, and she named herself Mildred. As she matured, she professed to be an atheist and yearned to be an intellectual. She received her nurse's training in the 1930s and fell in love with a

Jewish doctor. They met at the Williard hospital in Chicago.

Mil wrote a passage that she titled "Our Dreams" in a black three-ring book she kept. This list of dreams was created sometime in the 1930s:

1. *To see Athens, Singapore, Venice, London, Taj Mahal, Hawaii, the Congo, Mexico —together.*

2. *To have, somewhere, some time, a place that we can call "Our joint," furnished with curios from our wanderings, and flocks of books, and an "Atlas" and a microscope, a radio, and a pot of vile coffee always on the stove.*

3. *A car, any old kind, so we can, on flaming October days, explore bumpy country roads and all those "g-d alleys that aren't on the map."*

4. *Work that will make us happy and keep us busy and make us useful.*

   Right now life is one Grand Depression in finances, spirits, plans, hopes,—in everything. The only thing left are dreams and you. As long as we continue dreaming together, continue making second-hand coffee and laughing at ping-pong tables, and arguing about nothing, I'll survive.

   Dearheart, I hope you never change.

Mildred's mom, Isabella Del Re, my dumpling of a great grandmother, lived in Chicago. She was a widow. I don't know what happened to her husband Paul Formento. I have a picture where he is in looking out from a rough balcony with wooden stairs in a strange tenement looking building in Chicago. I guess this is where my grandmother grew up.

Jewish Doctor Morrie Lipstein ended up married to my grandmother, Mildred Formento, the beautiful, Italian, peasant nurse with strong genes and a good mind. Their wedding anniversary is January 1, 1938. After they married, they spent some time in Chicago together, then my grandfather entered the Indian Service, and in 1939, my dad, Paul Albert Lipton was born on the Sioux Indian reservation in Rosebud, South Dakota.

Then in 1941, my Uncle Dan was born in Watsonville, California and the family moved in Stockton, which was close to Morrie's cousin Irving Goleman and his wife Fay Goleman nee' Weinberg.

Then came World War II.

My grandfather was working to become a Flight Surgeon with the Army Air Corps and was stationed at *Stockton Army Air Field*. Then he was deployed, departing from Stockton on October 27, 1942 on a train for Los Angeles.

At this time, Morrie's mother, Rose Lipton lived in Los Angeles near the La Brea Tar Pits in the Jewish section. Al Lipton, her younger son lived in Dallas.

Morrie took the route from Stockton, to Los Angeles, to Dallas, to New Orleans, on his way to Foreign Service. The first letter I have in my possession is written on stationery from *Bullock's* ◆ *Broadway* ◆ *Hill* ◆ *Seventh*— Los Angeles, California–Fourth Floor Lounge.

The correspondence between Morrie and Mildred began October 28, 1942.

FROM MORRIE TO MIL

October 28, 1942

Los Angeles, Ca.

Couldn't sleep last night thinking of you and the kids, finally managed 4 hours. Train was 3 hours late…Mom (Rose) and Jewel met me at the depot. I managed to get sleepers to Dallas, so expect I will manage all right… I do love you and miss you so. Will write again real soon. Write to me c/o Al.

Love, Morrie

FROM MIL TO MORRIE

Thurs. October 29th 1942

Stockton, Ca.

Your letter arrived in this afternoon's mail…Paul said I should tell you he misses you and you are supposed to send him a cap gun. I reminded him that he was too young, but he isn't impressed…The Halloween Party is the all-consuming topic amongst all the children, even the older ones, so I'm glad I got the idea of having one. I also asked Irving to bring Deborah if he didn't think it was too much trouble…I took Paul to Dr. Miller, chiropodist, who said I should continue soaking that foot and to keep a sort of poultice on it of equal parts glycerine and alcohol. He advised getting shoes at least one inch longer than necessary, which I did. The poor child is really all feet and

even trips over them quite often, but is so proud of having shoes

"bigger'en the world"

…The new Harper's came…read the first article dealing with

the Battle of the Java Sea. The Houston was lost without a

trace, and it seems it is just possible that the crew escaped to

either Sumatra or Java – which in itself would probably be

horrible, if all the talk about Jap cruelty is true. Hope you can

read my writing. I'll get a new ribbon and type from now on.

And so the correspondence began and still remains tangible. I have in boxes, the daily thoughts of my grandparents from 1942 to 1945. I promised Fay Goleman at her 98th birthday that I would be sure the letters ended up with a library somewhere.

Morrie continued on to New Orleans. It was from here that he would leave the country.

FROM MORRIE TO MIL

November 12, 1942

Casual Officers Detachment NOSA, New Orleans, La.

Dearest One:

This, my sweet is a love letter to you. I haven't written one in

a long time, have I? But you know that I love you more than

I can ever tell you, don't you? Do you know that you are an

inseparable part of me – that you complete me – that I worship you? Thank you for giving me the happiest years of my life, the joy of being with you, the pleasure of your wonderful body, and the two most wonderful boys in the world. Thank you for your loyalty, and encouragement, and your love and devotion. I hope that I have in some small measure indicated to you what I owe you — and that I have been a good husband to you. Tonight I finished packing my equipment. There is a good possibility that I may leave in the very near future, perhaps tomorrow. If not, I will wire you and ask you to come here for a few days.

… Tonight we are alerted and as I explained in my previous letter, no communication is permitted from the outside. If I do not leave, I will let you know. How are Paul and Danny? How was the trip? How is Ma? [Rose] Write soon. Love to all

—Morrie

―

*F*ROM **M**IL TO **M**ORRIE

November 12, 1942

Dallas to New Orleans

Your wire came tonight — I feel that I can interpret it only one way. Happy sailing, my dearest, wherever you go, my heart goes with you.

And in the margin she wrote:

How do you like N.O.? What have you seen of it? What

strange foods have you had? How's your morale?

At the time, my grandmother could not know where my grandfather had been sent. She and the two boys, Paul and Dan were stuck on trains, rambling from Stockton to Dallas, then on to Chicago, where Mil's mother Isabella lived.

FROM MIL TO MORRIE

November 16, 1942

Dallas, Tx.

Now I'll tell you about my plans. I wasn't going to Chicago

because I dreaded the cross continental trip alone with the

children, but Mom (Isabella) wrote and said she feels so badly

about your being away, that she will spend the winter and

perhaps longer in Stockton with me...I'll go from here to

Chicago soon after Thanksgiving...get my Mom organized and

we'll hightail it back to Stockton around the middle of Dec. for

fear of getting stuck in Chicago for the duration.

From Dallas, Mil had the chance to write to Fay and Irving back in Stockton. She told of the rough journey from Stockton to Dallas by train.

From Mil to Fay and Irving Goleman

November 20, 1942

Dallas, Tx.

Dear Fay and Irving,

I haven't written sooner for two reasons. One was that the trip was so awful it took us nearly four days to get over it and the second is that Ma [Rose] has been quite ill, probably as a result of all the excitement and tension and the trip, etc. ...We feel we should not have made the trip. I thought...that it would help me over a rough period, but I find that I spend as many hours crying here as I would have in Stockton. I had so hoped I might see Morrie again, that when his wire came saying, "don't come – love and good-bye", it caught me off guard. ...We hear from many sources that civilian transportation is going to be curtailed drastically soon...From our trip, we know that something drastic will have to be done about civilian activity...the railroad simply can't handle it all. We had exactly five meals from the diner in four days travelling [from Stockton to Dallas]. I got so sick of soggy bread and salmon patties and canned stuff, I stopped eating. The children were asking for food constantly, since they didn't get a full meal. Four of the five meals were breakfasts, and it took over an hour to get oatmeal, milk, toast and coffee. One morning, the children ate their cereal without milk or sugar because we just didn't get it until we were all through eating.

That didn't kill them of course, but that gives you an idea of

what it was like. No civilian could hope to get lunch till about

4 pm, which was when the soldiers all finally got fed. They also

had a car full of Japanese evacuees who got fed first... Hope

you've all been well...Love from all of us

—*Mil*

⸺

*F*ROM MORRIE TO MIL

December 10, 1942

APO 811–Dakota Field, San Nicholas

Aruba, Netherlands West Indies

Here I am at my final destination at last... The living

accommodations are not very swell and the food is far from what

I could desire, but I think I can make it do...APO 811 is not

owned by the United States and American money is not accepted

here for anything...Is your mother with you? I hope so. Give

her a good big kiss for me.

December 1942 rolled on and my grandmother Mil came home to
Stockton with her mom Isabella, Paul, and Danny. Mil set up a room for
her mother, and she shared the other bedroom with Paul and Danny. Paul
was nearly four years old and Danny was about one and a half. Christmas
preparations were underway and Auntie Vi, Mil's younger sister, would
visit from San Francisco and Rose Lipton would come up from
Los Angeles.

From Mil to Morrie

December 22, 1942

Stockton, Ca.

Ma [Rose] *wrote to me that she would be up tomorrow night. I suppose the train will be crowded, poor thing, but I do really want her here, and I think she is pleased to know I do, as there was no further argument about that seat being needed by a soldier... Vi will be here Thursday night and Paul can hardly wait, not because he is so anxious to see her, but because I told him first came Auntie Vi, and then came Santa Claus. He is really impatient for Christmas to come and loves his tree so much... It is lovely, reaches clear up to the ceiling; in fact I had to cut off a few inches in order to put a silver star on top. That was the only thing I bought... as I still had everything from last year including the tinsel. Danny loves the tree too and crawls into the lower branches- he looks like a fat happy elf peering out from there. You would be amazed at his vocabulary... He made such a mess feeding himself one day that I said, "My, aren't you dainty?" Ever since then he says dainty when he means mess.*

From Morrie to Mil

Dec 27, 1942

APO811—Aruba, Netherlands West Indies

...We had a nice Christmas dinner here at camp: cake, cookies,

nuts, cigarettes, turkey pie, etc. I go to the outdoor movie every

night...last night I saw the Wizard of Oz. In it, at the end,

Dorothy taps the heels of her ruby slippers together and says,

"There's no place like home" and presto, home she is. It does

not work with either pair of the shoes I have...I hope the

bedbugs are quiet tonight. I have had two bad sieges with them.

How did the kids react to the tree? Did they like the gifts? How

are you getting along with the meat shortage?...Write to me

soon and often. Love

—Morrie.

On December 30, 1942 Morrie sent news of his transfer to
APO687, Edinburgh Field, Trinidad. Both mothers, Rose and Isabella
stayed in the little house in Stockton for the holidays with Mil and the
boys.

FROM MIL TO MORRIE

Jan 1, 1943

Stockton, Ca.

...We've been having a time about the heat - you know how

she [Isabella] freezes and how your mother [Rose] burns...

We're having the tribe for dinner Sunday and having goose -

almost criminal for me to tell you about it, isn't it? – with all the

wonderful schmaltz —ummh! I bought a lovely wool comforter

*for Paul and he has been sleeping much better — I think all
the other blankets weighed him down…Mama [Isabella] uses
eight blankets, her heavy coat and a boiling hot water bottle and
giggles when she remembers how you used to say she would
squash.*

From Morrie to Mil

Jan 3, 1943

APO687 Edinburgh Field, Trinidad

*I finally arrived at this station [APO687] yesterday…The
food is very much better, more variety, more nicely served and
damn few flies. I have a nice large room…a roommate whom I
have not yet seen, and a table. No chair. And no bedbugs. We
have a little hospital here of about 50 beds — the equipment is
not complete, but we can manage to do a number of things. I am
the base surgeon and in command as the ranking officer. There
are five other medical officers and two dentists. The setup is quite
nice and the living is much less rugged than it was…What is
new at Stockton? How are the Golemans? Write often and at
great length. Because I feel that each letter is a part of you, sent
to me, and since that is all I can have now, it is very important.
…Kiss the boys for me. All my love to you, my sweet. Kiss
Mom. Love*

—Morrie.

FROM MIL TO MORRIE

Jan 10, 1943

Stockton, Ca.

*Downtown I bought some new shades for the children's room.
Dan had managed to tear those to shreds, then I went to the
butcher and from there…to Fay's. I was feeling especially low
- I had Paul with me so decided that a talk with either one or
both of the G[oleman]'s wouldn't hurt. Upshot is we stayed
for lunch, had a nice visit. I really feel that Fay is listening to
me now, and that when she asks a question it is because she
does want to know the answer to it. She is assiduously clipping
out a daily column from the S.F. Chronicle entitled "So your
husband's gone to war" for me. Irv seemed pleased that I had
stopped in and in fact both of them urged me to do it oftener…
They were here for dinner yesterday – Mama [Isabella] had
made bread the day before – the first time since we got here -
and of course pizza. I still had some schmaltz so we feasted
– pizza, fresh crusty bread with schmaltz – till we could hardly
move. We all thought of you with each mouthful…I told them
about how Dan bopped Ruth Brodsky's child and Irv laughed
until he choked about the whole thing.
…Oh yes, a heartbreaking letter came from the local Hadassah
saying if they can raise $5000 they can take 700 Jewish
children out of the various occupied countries of Palestine -*

everything is arranged except the money, so of course I sent $5.

—Mil

———

FROM MORRIE TO MIL

Jan. 10, 1943

APO687 Edinburgh Field, Trinidad

The commanding officer here is a hell of a swell Joe – although he is a disciple of the body beautiful. He has ordered that all officers take physical exercise every morning in order to build up for a commando exercise, the structure for which is being erected now. This is sort of a monstrous jungle gym with thirty-foot ropes and bars and ladders and poles, etc. The completion of the exercise in the commando course takes two hours of violent exercise. Judging from the effects of the morning exercises on me, I hope that by the time the Commando course is finished that I have some mild disease such as malaria of the blackwater type or bubonic plague or something of like nature.

…I have a number of congenial men to work with, but there is one SOB here that is the proverbial fly in the ointment. I have had to put him in his place on several occasions and I shall request his transfer if he does not improve…I am glad that Paul remembers me so vividly and I hope that he always will. I don't expect that Danny will but then he is such a little fellow.

…Have you heard the song, "I'm dreaming of a White

Christmas"? Well I have been told that the theme song around these parts is "I'm dreaming of a White Mistress." I'm still dreaming of you my sweet and I always will... Morrie

~

FROM MIL TO MORRIE

Jan 13, 1943

Stockton, Ca.

Mama [Isabella] is fine as long as Dan is up and around, she has eyes for nothing else. She and Paul are great friends but Dan is her heart. He surely takes advantage of it too. I'm all right physically, but not mentally and won't be till you get back here to stay. No use going into that any deeper...

~

FROM MORRIE TO MIL

Jan 18, 1943

APO687 Edinburgh Field, Trinidad

Sweet, I know that you are lonesome for me, but you must not let yourself get depressed. I get lonesome too and I have 3 to be lonesome for...

I did not get the letter from Dallas in which you tell of Danny bopping Ruth Brodsky's child. I am very much interested in hearing of the episode. Remembering Ruth Brodsky and her husband, I feel that Danny must be a child of rare intelligence

and discernment to bop their offspring…Keep your chin up my
dear — you are doing a wonderful job with the kids and I am
very proud of you… Love Morrie

—

From Mil to Morrie

Jan. 19, 1943

Stockton, Ca.

Dearest Morrie,

Dan gets to be bigger every day and more adult in his
understanding too. He makes short sentences such as, "turn on
da wite", "pooey in da pants", "gink of vater"…he runs little
errands after which he says of himself "goo - boy". He is a
honey. Paul has many more interests now. He will spend quite
some time with his painting, though I confess I think it is the
water that intrigues him most. I don't scold when he spills and
makes a mess and between the two of them my mop is kept in
pretty constant use… He uses his black board and likes to use a
scissors. He builds with his various block sets too, so you can see
his scope is wider. However, he still likes his books best of all.
Mama [Isabella] *favors Dan of course, but it doesn't seem as*
bad as last year and they are good friends…

—Mil

—

From Mil to Morrie

Jan 24, 1943

Stockton, Ca.

…Paul was delighted to have your picture and took it to bed with him. They are both well and happy and Paul keeps talking about different things you did "before you went away" He is quite matter of fact and tells me you won't be back till the war is over and all the Japs and Hitler and Mussowienie are dead. He also talks about what you and he will do together when you get back. For instance, you'll go for a long, long ride and buy many oranges, and I'll have to stay home, and I won't get any oranges. He also says you'll take him for a ride in an airplane and he insists… you will bring him a cap gun. Of this I cannot dissuade him…with love from us all, especially me

—Mil

From Morrie to Mil

Jan 27, 1943

APO687 Edinburgh Field, Trinidad

Yesterday I went into town and I saw some nice trinkets, which I bought for you. I bought them from an Indian — an ivory elephant and an elephant bell. The bell is a magic one — when it is rung the magic number of times I will return to you. I do not know what the number is, but if you ring it once a day — on the day the magic number is rung, I will return to you.

...got two letters from you this evening, one dated Nov 19...with the pictures of the kids and the episode of Danny bopping Ruth Brodsky's kid. ...Paul is becoming more self sufficient from the way you describe his actions with paints and blocks, etc. and I think that maybe for his fifth birthday, he should have an electric train. That is provided I am home to play with it. Danny is coming along very well...What does pooey in da pants mean? — does it mean what I think it means?...Your letter sounded so cheerful — and I think that it was the result of your peasant heredity — nothing like digging in the garden and throwing a little manure around to make you feel good.

...they had a USO show here last night — a pretty good magician, a fair comedian and three girls direct from Minsky's burlesque. The latter of course were the hit of the show with the boys here. I enjoyed the thing although it was very corny. So far have received no mail from Vi or from Irv and Fay. I almost hope Irv doesn't write so I can feel justified in my forecast when I left Stockton. I say that in fun however, as I really would like to hear from them... Love

—Morrie.

CHAPTER 10

CARIBBEAN DEFENSE COMMAND

——

What was the reason my grandfather was sent to Dakota Field, San Nicholas, Aruba in late 1942? Thanks to William C. Gaines and Lew A. Dew, I was able to get the answer to this question in the broad retrospective view.

Lee A. Dew, tells the story in his article, "The Day Hitler Lost the War," published in the *American Legion Magazine*, February 1978. William C. Gaines documented these events in his article: "The United States Coast Artillery Command on Aruba and Curaçao in World War II."

The reason my grandfather, Dr. M.L. Lipton went to Aruba during World War II is because of oil. In the 1920's, oil was discovered in the Lake Maracaibo Basin of Venezuela. The oil companies were reluctant to risk dealing with the unstable Venezuelan government, so they built their refineries on the small islands of Aruba and Curaçao. When the war in Europe began in 1939, the strategic importance of the refineries at Aruba and Curaçao increased. The refinery at San Nicolas, Aruba was the world's largest refinery at the time and produced mainly aviation gasoline and motor fuels. The U.S. War Department ordered the defense of Aruba and Curaçao by the Caribbean Defense Command.

On the other side, the Aruba refinery was considered an important target for the Germans. The refinery was the primary source of fuel for the Royal Air Force and the British Eighth Army guarding the Suez Canal. If the fuel supply to the British Eighth Army were cut off, then Rommel's Afrika Korps could take Alexandria, occupy the Suez Cannel and continue into the Middle East.

German U-boat Commander, Werner Hartenstein set out as part of the Neuland Gruppe, which included five German U-boats and two Italian submarines on the mission that he believed would turn the war irrevocably in favor of Germany. On January 19, 1942, Hartenstein left from Lorient, France and piloted his Unterseeboot, the U-156, southwest into the Atlantic Ocean.

At dusk, on February 13, 1942, Commander Hartenstein surfaced the U-156 off the southeastern point of Aruba. He saw the lighthouse at Ceru Colorado and then came around to a position off the harbor of San Nicholas. The refinery was bright, lit up in the night, operating at full capacity, helpless. Hartenstein saw four large tankers in the port and another three anchored in the roadstead.

He submerged the U-156 and planned the attack. Destroying the tankers was important, but the main target was the refinery itself. Hartenstein's plan was to torpedo any tankers that seemed like easy targets, and then shell the refinery with the 105 mm cannon mounted on the U-156.

The refinery tank farm would be easy to hit from a distance of 1500 meters, and the cannon fire would ignite the huge stores of aviation gasoline in the refinery tanks, which would pour into the refinery area, forming a tremendous fireball of destruction. The U-156 artillery officer: Lieutenant Dietrich A. von dem Borne was in charge of the 105 mm cannon.

Late at night, on February 16, 1942, the U-156 surfaced off the San Nicholas roadstead, ready to attack. This night was the culmination of five months of intensive preparation by Hartenstein, the crew of U-156, and Lieutenant von dem Borne.

The tankers SS Pedernales and SS Oranjestade were anchored in the roadstead and the tanker Arkansas was moored to the San Nicholas wharf.

The crew of U-156 prepared for combat. Lee A. Dew tells the story in his article: *The Day Hitler Lost the War.*

...Lt. von dem Borne directed the gunnery crews in readying their 105 mm and 37 mm guns and the 30 mm antiaircraft gun. Lt. Just, below, prepared the torpedoes. Hartenstein studied his prey, lying unsuspecting in the distance. Zero hour approached. Carefully Hartenstein maneuvered his boat into position on the surface. The silhouette of the Pedernales was outlined clearly against the lights on shore. The order was given—the torpedo sped towards its target, striking the tanker amidships. The log of U-156 told the story: 0831 (Berlin Time) Surface shot at tanker—detonation after 48.5 seconds. Tanker burned immediately. Two

minutes later another torpedo shattered the tanker Oranjestad, anchored, like the Pedernales, in the roadstead of the harbor awaiting clearance to unload its crude oil. Burning oil quickly spread around both ships. Crewmen scrambled toward lifeboats or jumped from slanting decks into the sea. Shouts and screams echoed across the fire lit water. Hartenstein, cool and precise as always, ordered a change of course to 300 degrees. U-156, still on the surface, moved along the coastline until it was immediately opposite the refinery, three-fourths of a mile off the barrier reef. The gun crews stood ready, and, at von dem Borne's order, slammed the first shell into the breach of the 105. The refinery and its hundreds of storage tanks were a massive target-there was no way they could miss. "Fire," von dem Borne shouted, and the cannon exploded in a burst of flying metal. One crewman lay on the deck, mortally wounded. Von dem Borne, one foot a mass of bloody tissue and splinters of bone, was slammed backward against the base of the conning tower. What had gone wrong? A crewman dashed toward the conning tower with a report, in response to Hartenstein's shout of rage. The round had detonated in the cannon barrel. Someone had failed to remove the muzzle plug, which kept salt water out of the barrel when the boat was submerged. The cannon was useless, its barrel splayed and twisted. It was that close a thing! Had it not been for the carelessness of an unknown German sailor, U-156 might have blown the world's largest refinery right out of the war.

One year later, my grandfather wrote to my grandmother from this place, this part of the world that had, by fate and luck, strategy, action, and foolishness, been a fulcrum on which the balance of the war teetered. Cool. It was obvious that the Caribbean refineries needed to be defended, and my grandfather was part of that effort as a Flight Surgeon in the Army Air Corps. But after the incident with the U-156, the area did not see much action beyond the lone wolf hunting techniques of the German U-boats. No serious attempt was made again to shell the refineries. The troops there became frustrated and restless, feeling like they had been relegated to a backwater region. He also serves, who waits.

FROM MORRIE TO MIL

Jan 28, 1943

APO687 Edinburgh Field, Trinidad

…I've been sitting here thinking about the happy times that I have had with you. I remember the evening I met you at the Williard – how trim and nice and attractive you seemed to me – and how you bawled me out for making a nincompoop of myself even though you did not know me and how I took it because I liked you so very well even five minutes after I met you. And I remember the walks to your home from the hospital, and the beer we drank and the stories I told you and the trips to the World's fair and the musical fountain and the A & P exhibit with their gypsies and the evening up in Mollie's room when you told me you were engaged to Johnnie what's his name and how I told you that you would never marry him – because you were too vital and too nice for him and how you told me, "wait and see".

I remember the letters you wrote to me in Michigan and how you helped me shop for my first suit and top coat when I was in

Chicago en route to New Mexico and the letters you wrote me

in New Mexico and how you stopped writing and how I almost

stopped breathing when I no longer got your letters. And then

you started writing again and I started living again. I remember

my visits to you in Fresno and how you came to L.A. and our

trips to the ocean and the swell hamburgers we ate at night and

how I loved you long before I ever realized I did.

I remember when you came to San Diego and how we shopped

for your wedding dress and hat – and I remember the books

you brought along for me. You must have been on a merry

go round when you picked them for me – and I remember

that you did not like the hat after you had it for a while. I

remember the night that Paul was born and how you felt sorry

for me because I was in such mental anguish and I remember

the ride to Fort Ord and how Danny was almost born in Salt

Lake City. I remember the pleasant evenings we spent together

playing rummy and all the lovely nights we have had together. I

remember how you walk and talk and smile and how lovely you

are and how much I love you…

Enough of reminiscing…Nothing very important happens here

and the days are the same – one after the other. Love

—Morrie

FROM MIL TO MORRIE

Jan 30, 1943

Stockton, Ca.

…how goes the calisthenics? …Yesterday Paul said, apropos of

nothing, "When Daddy comes home he surely will be hungry."

How true, thought I. I think Paul was hungry too at the time.

—

FROM MORRIE TO MIL

Jan 30, 1943

APO687 Edinburgh Field, Trinidad

…I waited for the mail to come in at 4:30 and since no m ail came in

I felt very blue and de pressed and I started drinking. I am as a matter

of fact quote drunk and maybe it is a good think as I will probably be

able to sleep tonight…You are my sweet and my darling and my only

one and I hope this godamn war ens soon so I can come home and be a

normal human being again…I've been drinking steadily since 4:30…

but then the e is always tomordow anc I hope tha I get aletrwr frm you

then. If not I wil, get drunk again and that is a bad thing. If you do

not believe me read Somersst Mauthm. Drinking anf the tropics is a bad

thing. There is somehti g, wrong with thiw typewrite as the letters seem to

get stuck togethet and I do not ;ike iti. I think I will ha e this typewriter

xcondemened…

All my love —Morrie

*F*ROM MIL TO MORRIE

Feb 21, 1943

Stockton, Ca.

…you reminded me of that set of books I gave you as a wedding present…and how you said I must have been on a merry go round. I can still remember buying those books – going in and asking for something a well-read gentleman would enjoy owning. The salesman recommended those highly, so without looking at them I had them wrapped up. Perhaps I shouldn't have said "Gentleman" and he might have given me something you really would have enjoyed… I had to laugh again, thinking of them, and also of that hat I never liked and finally gave to Candida as the felt was too good to just throw the thing out… Do you remember how you had to buy me a sour pickle every time we went to that particular shop in San Diego because I was drooling so, I couldn't even ask for them?

…Do you remember driving me through Christmas tree lane in Fresno?

…Remember how much time and effort you spent rigging up that darn pump in the bathroom in Wood, and we had to pump forty strokes when it would have been much simpler to have used the outhouse in the first place? And how we bathed in the basement, sluicing water over each other? My darling – do you remember how you left me in the car for five minutes outside the

post office and when you came back I was ravenously devouring sour olives and tearing off great hunks of bread and fishing anchovies out of a can and I was grease from ear to ear and beaming at you?

...Did I tell you that Irving was down at the station the night Mom left? After the train pulled out...I suggested that we go have some coffee and he sort of hesitated so I said if he'd rather go right on home just say so, after all we were somehow related. So he said, he would love coffee but he had only two bits with him. After we got in the restaurant I slipped a four bit piece to him under the counter and he said he was the kind of guy who would take it over the counter too, so that reminded me of you, and how you always gave me a couple of bills when we were coming out of some hotel or some such place. He laughed and said he was even worse because when he and Fay were in New Haven and went into New York for an overnight stay, coming down in the hotel elevator he would comment to Fay, "That was very nice, well worth two dollars." Till she put a stop to that as I did the other.

ℱROM MORRIE TO MIL

March 7, 1943

APO687 Edinburgh Field, Trinidad

…Did you have a nice time in S.F. and did you get everything

that you wanted to get? Did you eat at Cathay House?

During these years, my grandfather, Morrie had a fitful correspondence with his cousin, Irving. Morrie was a steady writer, but Irving's letters to Morrie were few and far between. In response to a scarce letter from Irving in 1943, Morrie wrote the following:

—

ℱROM MORRIE TO IRV AND FAY

March 7, 1943

APO687 Edinburgh Field, Trinidad

Dear Irv and Fay,

Received your letter several days ago – I received it with

intermingled emotions. I was not sure if pleasure from receiving

a letter from you balanced the pleasure of being angry with you

for not writing. However, after I read your letter, I was glad that

you had written.

I have very little to write about – the greatest curse of this war

to me is boredom. I have very little to do and plenty of time in

which to do it. The recreational facilities are very limited and so

I have a great deal of time in which to sit and bemoan my fate.

Reading material is scarce as hen's teeth… I have been able to
get number of the paper backed two bit books to read. The latest
one that I have read is Elmer Gantry. Luckily, I read it just at
the time that I was so bored that I was even going to go to the
services of the Chaplain this morning. However, after reading
Elmer Gantry, I decided to stay at home and be bored. …Your
experience on the bus with Deborah reminded me of an incident
that occurred shortly after Mil and I were married. We drove
to the store to pick up some groceries and supplies, and we took
with us the little daughter of a neighbor – a girl about 6 years
of age. While at the store, I saw toilet paper on sale – 6 rolls for
$.49 or something like that, and I picked up the six rolls and
carried them over to the counter. Little Nancy in her clear piping
voice called out so the whole store full of people could hear, "Oh,
Doctor – are you going to use all of those?"
I hope that you liked Chauncey Leakes lecture; I think he is
a very fine speaker and a very clear thinker. The fact that the
Russians are turning out six times as many doctors as we are
shows that they have been markedly understaffed in this field
in Russia. I do not think that the US could use as many as
6 times the doctors that they have now, unless we go in for
socialized medicine and guarantee a living wage to all doctors.
I think the AMA [American Medical Association] *got what*
it deserved. I approve of the clinic form of medicine and this

particular form of socialized medicine, in order that the middle class may get the proper medical care which is now available only to the very rich and the very poor.

…Glad that your mother [Ida Goldman] managed to ship Aunt Bertha [Bertha Levin] away because I really think that she is a vixen.

Glad that you are feeling better Irving and do not forget that a man is only as old as he feels. After all, you are not so terribly much older than I am and I feel in the pink of condition physically. I am very lonesome for Mil and the children and I will never be really happy until I get back to them and resume a normal life again. Thanks for your letter and all the nice things you said about my wife and children. I accept them at full face value because I know they are true.

Regards to all, Love

—Morrie

⬱

From Mil to Morrie

March 9, 1943

Stockton, Ca.

Paul tells me we mustn't waste food because of the war, and he really seems to believe it himself for he cleans his plates. I am out of paper towels and he wanted one today so I said we didn't have any. "Can't you buy any more, Mom?" I said I thought

I could get some at the store, so he said, "Yes, you can get them because the soldiers don't wash their hands, they mostly wipe them on the grass".

~

FROM MORRIE TO MIL

March 11, 1943

APO687 Edinburgh Field, Trinidad

I have just finished writing letters to Mom – Rolla – and Larry. I received letters from them last night and since it is my policy to carry unanswered letters around with me until I answer them and since I do not have too many pockets I sat down this afternoon and answered them. Rolla enclosed a picture of her husband and the baby. The baby is a very happy healthy looking youngster. He looks like Rolla, which is, I think a very good thing.

~

FROM MIL TO MORRIE

March 18, 1943

Stockton, Ca.

…Paul was very pleased to get a letter from you but refuses to dictate one to you – I don't know why… The books I got for him are "Friendly Little Jonathan", "Nobody's Mouse" (he likes that best), "Mike Mulligan and his Steam Shovel… You should

see his bookcase – it is filled with books, even Deborah doesn't have so many. As for Danny…he isn't interested in books yet… He still tears them to shreds, too. He is so proud to be sleeping in the big bed instead of the crib now. This afternoon, Vi and I were both very quiet, we were fixing her skirt, when suddenly the door opened and there stood Danny. For a split second I forgot he was in the bed instead of the crib and was almost frightened to see him standing there, but I remembered right away and the same thing happened to Vi, so we both exclaimed at once, "Well, good morning, look who's here." That was such a royal welcome, for he had to do it again, in fact, he crawled in bed four more times, covered himself and each time I had to close the door. Then he hopped out again and we both had to be amazed at him.

—

FROM MORRIE TO MIL

March 19, 1943

APO687 Edinburgh Field, Trinidad

Those monkeys of ours seem to be keeping you busy – but they are a lot of fun. I believe you will have to extricate Danny from many things into which his exuberance will get him. It seems strange that [Paul] a four year old can make an adult feel inferior. He does have a very sane and steady opinion of himself. He is a honey. He is just Paul and that is the best thing that *could be… We had a USO show last night with Pat O'Brien*

of movie fame. It was very good — lots of stories and rope tricks

and jokes and a few dramatic recitations — I enjoyed it. We get

them about once every 6 weeks. Will write at greater length

tonight or tomorrow, Love,

—Morrie

From Mil to Morrie

March 21, 1943

Stockton, Ca.

I do miss you so much Morrie. I try not to let myself think of it, but

today when Churchill said the war might last 2 or 3 more years, I really

got depressed. I love you with all my heart.

—Mil

CHAPTER 11

MORE WAR CORRESPONDENCE

—

FROM MORRIE TO MIL

March 21, 1943

APO687 Edinburgh Field, Trinidad

I have just returned from a visit to an overseer of a sugar

plantation and listened to some fascinating stories of Voodoo

practice, which goes on here. They have, instead of what the

Haitians call Zombies, Jombies – and human vampires and

charms and love poultices, etc.

—

FROM MIL TO MORRIE

March 23, 1943

Stockton, Ca.

…when I talk of going to S.F., I feel guilty somehow, as I know

how much you like the city and how much you would enjoy a

trip there again. You'd find the place changed, though. You'd

not find such a cosmopolitan air about it – you would sense the

tremendous work that is being done there, and see evidence of

it in the men and women going about in working clothes, and

guards stationed everywhere, of many restaurants closed down,

of candy shops open for a few hours a day only, and of pastry

shops showing mostly breads, etc. The blackouts didn't do much

to sober that place, but rationing and scarcity has put the war

very close, and a good thing for most of us, say I. I don't think it

fair that the workers had to do without meat and butter, and still

do, as the meat situation there isn't improved yet, but I do think

the war effort got a tremendous boost. Did I tell you on my last

trip up there one department store showed a big placard saying,

"Please be kind to our salespeople; they are harder to get than

customers."?

My grandmother held down the proverbial fort in Stockton and
kept my grandfather informed about the happenings at home and at
Stockton Field. The March 17, 1945 edition of *The Twin Prop*—the official
weekly newspaper of Stockton Field during World War II, published the
article, "History of Stockton Field" by Sgt. Pete Pinkerton.

The first phase of Stockton Field's mission has been accomplished. And

behind the success of that mission lies a great story. In effect, it is the story of

America's progress in the air. It is the inspiring story of patriotic Americans, military and civilian alike, realizing the need for a gigantic air force, quickly

building a school to train thousands of the pilots who are today blasting the Axis

into oblivion. It is the almost-romantic story of the teaching of class after class of

cadets, maturing them into efficient, capable pilots, many of whose exploits, skill and

daring have won us victory in the skies the world over. Five years ago, [1940] a

small municipal airport was in business where Stockton Field now stands. At that

time there were a few civilian places on the stubby flight line and the only building

was an out-dated adobe hanger. From these meager surroundings, Stockton Field

grew to become the oldest advanced flying school in the Western Flying Training

Command. Today it is a vast installation with some three-score buildings drawn up

in neat, military lines.

—

*F*ROM MIL TO MORRIE

> *March 24, 1943*
>
> *Stockton, Ca.*
>
> *…then Franz went with me to the health center to have our*
>
> *blood typed and Wassermanned for blood bank donation. I've*
>
> *been wanting to do it for a long time and finally remembered*
>
> *to call yesterday… Ever since the night of that awful fire here,*
>
> *when you would finally talk about it, you said the plasma saved*
>
> *some lives, I have wanted to donate some blood… Tonight we*
>
> *meet Fay and Irving and go to the show. I don't much want to,*
>
> *but we'll go and then won't have to repeat that for a long time,*
>
> *I hope. I'd so much rather visit with them, either at our house*

or theirs, than for four adults to go to a show and then each go home and consider that a visit.

—

*F*ROM MORRIE TO MIL

March 24, 1943

APO687 Edinburgh Field, Trinidad

I have been very busy today – attended an autopsy, in fact assisted in it. I really enjoyed it, and though it was rather gruesome it was the first bit of anything professional that I have had to do since God knows when. I can tell you very little more, as it is censorable. Nothing to worry about, and really the result of an accident.

—

*F*ROM MIL TO MORRIE

March 25, 1943

Stockton, Ca.

…The boys are fine… Today, Vi started singing to Dan as he sat howling on the throne, "Oh dear, what can the matter be?" —Paul got a far away look in his eyes and said, "My daddy used to sing that song, long ago before he went away to the war."

—

CYNTHIA LIPTON

From Mil to Morrie

March 27, 1943

Stockton, Ca.

*This morning, Mrs. Beekman called to tell me that the two other
ladies, a Mrs. Wood and a Mrs. Matteson have decided that
since I do not have a car and therefore cannot do my share of
the chauffeuring, they don't want to be bothered coming around
the corner for Paul, to take him to nursery school… I was wild.
Ritchie Beekman lives around the corner, they are willing to
go for him, but don't care to drive ten houses down to pick up
another child, because in their stupid minds they have probably
figured out that this child is a nobody's child.*

*…I told her I will not be placed in a position of accepting favors
from women of that caliber. So – I've been ranting all day about
it – I've all but screamed to the high heavens that this boy, with
his father overseas trying to do as much as he can to protect our
way of life, should be denied, because of his fathers absence, the
privilege of attending school. I have had the whole neighborhood
in an uproar about the thing – and I'll keep shouting about it
until enough people will hear about that disgraceful thing, so
no one else will dare to do such a thing… everyone is [wild]
who hears about it, - and they think I should write to the paper
about it. I'm still too furious to do that – it would never see
print, but I do think that's a good way of being heard.*

Meanwhile in the tropics, my grandfather continued to wage war against boredom and insects.

FROM MORRIE TO MIL

March 28, 1943

APO687 Edinburgh Field, Trinidad

I went downtown the other day and bought some tape called Hoo Doo tape, which is supposed to keep the ants from passing it. I tied it to all the legs of my bed and so far there has been not one ant on it. That is a relief, as they were an awful nuisance to me.

FROM MIL TO MORRIE

March 31, 1943

Stockton, Ca.

I'm reading Werfel's "40 Days of Musa Dagh" – can you tell me who the Armenians are? Where they came from originally? Are they of Semitic origin? Werfel keeps saying, "Their eyes are big, big with a thousand years of terror." If they, as a race, have existed for that long, and have been persecuted during all that time, they must have Semitic origin… I hope you [know] or I'll have to make a trip to the library to find out. Some day I hope we'll own an Encyclopedia of our own for just such inquiries.

—

From Morrie to Mil

April 1, 1943

APO687 Edinburgh Field, Trinidad

Paul does remember his daddy, doesn't he? I almost cried when I read about Paul saying, "My Daddy used to sing that song long ago, before he went away to war." I love those children so that it feels that it almost amounts to idolatry... I wish you had taken a picture of Danny in his undershirt and pants and Indian headdress. He is such a fat little devil. Everyone seems to think he resembles me more than Paul does. Pretty soon he should start piddling like a man — but there is no hurry. He will be a man much longer than he will be a baby or a boy.

—

From Morrie to Mil

April 4, 1943

APO687 Edinburgh Field, Trinidad

...Two years ago tonight you were just waiting to get rid of your big tummy - and I was OD at Fort Ord. I remember that you called me in the morning and I got the day off to come and be with you — and then you presented Danny to me. Danny, that cheerful, fat rascal of a honey. He is such a monkey and I thank you for him.

—

FROM MORRIE TO MIL

April 5, 1943

APO687 Edinburgh Field, Trinidad

...I too was incensed over the selfishness of your good Christian

neighbors. Such people I am sure are the ones that go to church

on Sundays and forget all about their duties to their fellow man

on weekdays... If you get the opportunity to do so I suggest

that you write a little note to each of these fine ladies and thank

them for their courtesy in taking Paul to school for as often as

they have done so, and offer to reimburse them for any expense

they may have gone to. If they are not willing to accept any

money, why tell them that when I return from overseas, I will be

glad to take their children to school in my car until the great debt

to them has been repaid. Well, enough of that.

...I have not been over to see the overseer yet since my last trip,

and so I do not have any more lurid details to write to you

about. They have separate vampires — by name, one for the

female and one for the male, which I do not remember. But the

male one is the one that lives on the blood of females, and the

female one is the one that lives on the blood of the males. They

have what they call obeahs which are conjure bottles or bags

which contain all sorts of horrid things and are buried near the

home of a person whom they wish to charm or destroy... I have

told you in my previous letters that I got some tape called hoodoo tape which I have tied on the legs of my bed and the ants do not

crawl beyond the tape. It seems to work well — although I did

find a few ants in my bed tonight. I think they have crawled

on the ceiling of my room down the light fixture and down

the string I have attached to the switch and to my bed so that

I can turn out the light without crawling out of my mosquito

netting and bed. That is a complicated sentence, but I think you

understand it. I love you very very much and I would, of course,

much prefer to have you in my bed. I would not put a tape or a

conjure anywhere near it to keep you out. In fact, if I thought I

were losing you I would feed you some wet rice, which I will tell

you about when I return. That is a charm to make your loved

one return to you. Since I am confident that I will not need it I

did not get the exact proportions or formula for this.

FROM MIL TO MORRIE

April 8, 1943

Stockton, Ca.

…Yesterday was a real holiday for all of us. We celebrated Dan's

birthday at noon and he was sort or bewildered by the whole

thing. I put Dan to bed and he was prancing around, in and

out of the bed, and I was just going to put him in his crib when

Vi came… Rosemary finally did her shopping and came along

and all was hysterical from then on. Bronia was cracking nuts with such zip that nut shells were flying every which way…

I finally got the dishes washed, and got started on cookies for

the soiree and Rosemary helped, before long she was doing it

all. I made some sugared nuts and some filled cookies and some

plain cookies. Then Carol came along and took Paul out for a

haircut – over to a beauty parlor nearby where he got a good, fast

haircut for only 35 cents. When she came back from that I was

trying to make up an Alaska centerpiece, using our fur dolls as

the main attraction… we made a cardboard sleigh, with curved

runners… tied the woman doll into a small chair… inside the

sled, arranged cotton for the runway, Carol had some small bears

we also used, and she had a white reindeer we used on a hill of

cotton. The whole thing was really good, and filled the table, so

we hardly had room to put the food around.

…Irving came…after he finished his panel discussion on

"Education After the War"… Vi and Rosemary got off with

the help of all of us… Saturday morning, they leave by train

for Seattle. From there they go to Prince Rupert Island, and

then by boat to Skagway… There were no tears as it is quite

an adventure, and there is no cause for tears. Just before I put

Danny to bed tonight I gave the boys the presents for both of

them – Paul had the box for Rosemary, who was washing dishes,

and Dan the envelope to give to Vi, who was drying them. Paul

and Dan marched in solemn procession, bearing their gifts…

both girls were sort of weepy and touched, when Dan, who lingered a bit to see what was on the table, spied something, so he threw the envelope at Vi, said, "Here, Auntie Vi" and then pointing to the table, yelled, "Artichokes!"

... I made a dreadful mistake when I made him a devil's food cake for his birthday, but I felt it was quite appropriate to make an angel's food cake for Paul and a devil's food cake for Dan. He and the other boys spilled food all over the floor, cake included. I was rushing around doing something when I stepped on something. I looked and decided it was cake... As I wiped it off I realized my cake was drier than this — sure enough, it wasn't cake.

... You have thanked me for having presented you with Paul and Danny. ...I am glad we have them, they are tangible proofs of the love we bear each other. I am only sorry you aren't here to watch them grow — you are missing something, losing some part of them, but on the other hand, you are also missing the "is it cake or is it _ _ _ _?" stage, so maybe you aren't losing out too much.

From MORRIE TO MIL

April 10, 1943

APO687 Edinburgh Field, Trinidad

Dearest One,

... Well Danny's birthday has come and gone... I guess that Vee
has left for the cold parts of the world. She will probably get to
the southern part of Alaska and suffer this summer from the heat
and the mosquitoes... The days are getting very hot and muggy
– the evenings remain cool... Tonight we had a USO show –
several girls and men. I usually enjoy them not because they are
first rate but because they are flesh and blood actors. I get very
tired of the poor movies we have here.

From MIL TO MORRIE

April 13, 1943

Stockton, Ca.

... When you next sit around discussing prices of foods, here are
some more figures for you – five lousy, fibrous carrots cost 10
cents – squash is 35 cents a pound – tomatoes were 45 cents
for a while but are down to a mere 30 cents (remember how our
boys eat them with olive oil and vinegar, till they are ready to
pop?). Artichokes are around 12 cents each – strawberries were
45 cents a box (they are unseasonal as yet, but even so). Butter

is 60 cents a lb., first quality. Bacon at 52 cents per pound, to say nothing of the 8 points — the cheapest cut of meat for pot roast at 40 to 45 cents per lb. Well eating is practically a rich man's privilege these days — the point system democratizes it, but the prices don't. I can't help but wonder what difference there might be in prices if the Japanese farm workers had not been moved out. No white man is content with the small margin of profit the Japs got rich on.

CHAPTER 12

PASSOVER

—

FROM MORRIE TO MIL

April 14, 1943

APO687 Edinburgh Field, Trinidad

…Next Monday is the Passover and I have been invited by the Jewish
Chaplain to attend the Seder in the town being given by the Jewish
community here. Well of course you know how religious I am – but I am
going mainly because of the Jewish food I know will be served there…
Your description of Dan's party and the goodbye party for Vee and
Rosemary was very nice. I'll bet the centerpiece was very pretty.

—

FROM MIL TO MORRIE

April 15, 1943

Stockton, CA

Nothing sensational has happened here today to tell you about. I kept
puttering around all day long… I went over next door to get some roses

— saw that the bushes were all loaded with buds and blossoms so took all I wanted. Later on our neighbor across the street called over to ask if I wanted roses. It broke my heart to say no, but I really couldn't use any more. They are beautiful and the season for them is full on now... I'm only sorry my mother isn't here to enjoy them with me — she wouldn't say no if she had to use her pots and pans to put them in and have nothing to cook with...Had a letter from Peggy Dudenas today — she said they all took a two week course in chemical warfare and the nurses all acted as guinea pigs for a mustard gas attack. Result was that Peggy got two deep, bad burns on her arm that haven't healed yet... She said they've had nearly two thousand cases of scarlet fever since the first of the year — isn't that something?

—

*F*ROM MORRIE TO MIL

April 20, 1943

APO687 Edinburgh Field, Trinidad

...I went to the Seder in town that was held by the Jewish Chaplain with the help of the Jewish ladies in town and I did not get back until about midnight. The Seder was very nice, the service was very impressive and the food was delicious — Gefullte Fish, chicken soup with matzo dumplings, chicken and peas and carrots, fruit cup for dessert. Plenty of matzos, sacramental wine and some good company. The commanding officers of the various organizations mostly "Aryans" were present and expressed themselves as being very well pleased and honored to be there. I

am surprised to find so many Jewish boys in service here... Rae Romano

writes an interesting letter and says that Mom [Isabella] is planning to

come back to California for the duration. I hope so as I think you both

need each other...

—

From Morrie to Mil

April 20, 1943, 8:15 PM

APO687 Edinburgh Field, Trinidad

...I ordered some medical books tonight – Stitt's Tropical Medicine – and

it cost $21.00 and I have written a check for that amount... I told you

about going to the Seder last evening – I did not amplify on it. It has

been about 20 years since I went to a Seder and of course in those days

it had very little meaning to me – I am not getting religious, but I could

not help contrasting or rather comparing the ritual celebrating the passing

of the Jews from the land of Egypt and from tyranny with the situation

today. I hope that the next Passover will find us all – Jews and Catholics

and Protestants free of the misery of war and the tyranny of the dictator

nations and then the ritual of Passover will have a new meaning.

...I am determined to get out of debt and stay out of debt and still have

enough money so that we may be relatively independent regarding jobs.

I certainly do not wish to go into the Indian Service again and have the

same kind of deal we had the first time... I certainly wish to be able to

demand a hospital job... I am to attend a course given by some experts in

malaria and venereal diseases – the preventive side of the picture... and then I expect to really force our rate in both diseases down to rock bottom. It is a good thing to do and I will be glad if I can accomplish it.

From Mil to Morrie

April 21, 1943

Stockton, CA

Every day Paul seems to be developing more and more into a real boy. Today he came dashing into the house and went right to your tool chest and took your hammer. I didn't ask any questions – pretty soon I heard him pounding and still left him alone… I have consciously tried to let him do more of the things he wants to do, without always thinking of the mess he might make, or how he might hurt himself, or how I don't want to be bothered. He could have pounded his finger today, with your heavy hammer. But I guess he will do that many times before he can learn to handle it, so why shouldn't he start now?

…On the night when I took Paul and Dan to Fay's house… I met a young fellow named Joe Lorber – a vet, a nice Jewish boy… he was friendly and somehow different from their usual friends… A few weeks later Fay called to say she had a friend who had no use for his coffee stamp and would I be interested in swapping some canned food stamps with him for his coffee? I said yes. Some time later someone called and said he was Dr. Lorber. That didn't mean anything to me, so then he went on to explain he was the one I was going to swap with, and I had met him at Fay's… he told me he has a standing order with some

*butcher for liver and sweetbreads and would I like some… he called again
and said he would come out with the coffee and would also bring some
liver for me — nice and fresh… He ate like an adolescent boy — cleaned
up everything in sight so that it was a pleasure to watch him, and then
played with the boys — watched them have their baths, helped me with
the dishes, read to Paul, fixed the victrola attachment, found a dozen good
programs on the radio, and admired my garden… both Paul and Dan
screamed with joy when he carried them around on his shoulders like you
used to do… he was so nice I was glad he invited himself and in fact I
suggested that he come out on Mondays when Irving comes for dinner.*

FROM MORRIE TO MIL

April 22, 1943

APO687 Edinburgh Field, Trinidad

Dearest One:

*…How are you and how are the children? I am fine but a bit depressed
mentally; I am so damn lonesome for you I could almost cry. I suppose I
should not write these things to you but I can not help it… I do hope you
have been free of your headaches — I've never told you have I — how dear
you are to me — how much I love and worship you and how I would give
anything to be with you again — to have you welcome me with open arms
as I walk in through the door — Sweet you are everything to me — with
you I can do anything — without you I am nothing. Do not worry about
my depressive mood — we all get them here in fact they have a special*

name for it, the derivation of which I can not tell you, but we call it the

red ass. We always get over it in a day or two so it is not serious... Your

letters tomorrow will perk me up I am sure... Morrie

—

*ℱ*ROM MIL TO MORRIE

April 22, 1943

Stockton, CA

...I'll be busy tomorrow getting organized for Easter dinner... Bronia

went downtown today and bought the turkey for me — a 16 pound affair

that cost $7.90. Gone, gone are the days when we fed caponized turkey

to the Indians! By the time I get all the trimmings, this dinner will cost

me ten bucks, but I certainly owe them that much, so I don't mind really.

—

*ℱ*ROM MORRIE TO MIL

April 23, 1943

APO687 Edinburgh Field, Trinidad

I'm glad that you made Irv squirm. He deserves it. I know that I will

never get another letter from him and to tell you the truth, I don't much

care — You can quote me to that effect if you wish... darling do not think

that I don't know what a struggle it has been for you... but as long as

you love me and I love you... no corporeal separation can mar the beauty

of our marriage. When I return we'll try for a redheaded child. Kiss Paul

and Danny for me, and all my love to you darling.

—Morrie

> *April 25, 1943*
>
> *Stockton, CA*
>
> *Dear Morrie:*
>
> *Here I am already a whole day with Mil and the boys and I am really*
>
> *glad now that I came. Mil was so surprised, and genuinely pleased when*
>
> *she saw me that it warmed my heart... We had a very good dinner and*
>
> *your ears must have burnt, for we mentioned you many, many times.*
>
> *Let's hope that we all may be together next year and this horrible war a*
>
> *thing of the past. Love as ever*
>
> *—Ma*

I wish I had more from Rose, about Rose, to Rose. When I read the letters, I am reading my ancestors thoughts, exactly as those thoughts formed in their minds on the day they wrote them down. I get to know the feelings they felt day to day and how my dad and my uncle acted as little kids.

*F*ROM MIL TO MORRIE

> *April 27, 1943*
>
> *Stockton, CA*
>
> *This evening [Dan] and Paul were fighting over a book ... this was*
>
> *Paul's favorite book — the one about Mike Mulligan and the steam*
>
> *shovel... Dan took a good pounding... Dan put his right arm behind*

him as far as it would go and swung from way back there to let Paul

have a good one right in the face… Dan ran right after he socked Paul,

but Paul just settled back and listened again to Irv who all this time kept

right on reading aloud to Paul. Ma [Rose] and I went into the kitchen

and nearly had hysterics – over the fight, but also over Irv, with his two

gentle girls he didn't know how to handle the situation, so he just kept

right on reading and ignored the whole thing.

…My garden really is nice, though I'll admit it would be bigger and

better if Mom [Isabella] were here as she works by instinct with plants

and I don't. Everybody is yelling at me for watering my plants every

night – Ma [Rose] is scolding me for not having irrigation furrows

between the plants, Franz tells me this and Dorothy tell me that and Mrs.

Wise tells me the other, but I'm doing it the way I want, and the way I

remember my father did with his garden, than which there was no better,

and we'll see what we'll see. Meanwhile things keep growing, so I'm not

discouraged.

From Morrie to Mil

April 28, 1943

APO687 Edinburgh Field, Trinidad

I think your method of letting Paul do things for himself, and learning

things is very good. Even if he gets a smashed finger once in a while, it

will teach him to work with his hands and that I think is a very good

thing. Tell him I am very proud of him… Your friend Joe Lorber sounds very nice, but I must admit I felt a twinge of jealousy when I read about the dinner you had with him. Do not misunderstand me, my sweet, when I say I think you are wise in asking him to dinner when you have other people also...

—

From Morrie to Mil

April 29, 1943

APO687 Edinburgh Field, Trinidad

Dearest Darling;

Your April 23 letter came tonight... I wish I had the gift of words as you do so that I could tell you how very much I love and worship you. I want to apologize for being even a little bit jealous. I know that I have no cause for it and never will have and I feel ashamed that the thought of your having dinner with Joe made me feel jealous. But dear, the fact that someone else, whom I do not even know, can come in and play with my children and fix the victrola attachment in my house and have dinner with my wife, when I can't, made me feel my separation from you very keenly.

CHAPTER 13

STOCKTON TO CHICAGO

—

*F*ROM MIL TO MORRIE

May 1, 1943

Stockton, Ca

Yesterday Paul woke up at the crack of dawn asking if it was time to do to
the circus… The boys loved it and they'll probably play circus, for the rest
of the week, but I was glad it was over. If last year's was bad, this was
rotten. To help matters along, a fire broke out during the night before and
I guess all hands fell out to help fight the fire, so they were in no mood for
a performance. I never saw such uninspired clowns… We got out of the
big tent in time to hear the ballyhooer carry on about one of the sideshows,
and then, while we stood there, out came the snake lady with a snake
coiled about her, and the boys nearly fell over in excitement. When the
snake wiggled around and slithered into another coil around her middle,
their eyes were wide with a mixture of amazement and fear. That was
just exactly right for ending our stay there – when she went in, we left…

Today we go to the Goleman's for the day. Dan is all excited about

riding on the bus, and also about seeing "Judy punkin." Ma [Rose]

is going to take a good look at that gym set and will try to duplicate it

for our boys…I can't tell you how grand it is having your mother with

me. She took us by surprise so I didn't have a chance to get all steamed

up before she came. She came and she saw we do live like human beings

even when I'm not expecting her — well, I don't know why, but it is grand

having her, we are really good friends and I shall miss her and I think

she'll hate leaving us too.

Later on May 1, 1943

…Fay was very nice today — you know how nice she really can be when

she forgets she is Professor Goleman's wife…I was sort of relieved to see

that Deborah isn't the obedient paragon I sort of thought she was, that she

cries and carries on like Paul does once in a while.

FROM MIL TO MORRIE

May 3, 1943

Stockton, Ca

The Seder was all right but the food wasn't so hot — I did enjoy the wine.

I came in after it had started and in fact the book said, "Pour the second

glass of wine" so I moaned to Irving that I had missed the first and that

was a crime. I made up for it later — I think I had five altogether.

CYNTHIA LIPTON

ℱROM MORRIE TO MIL

June 25, 1943

APO687 Edinburgh Field, Trinidad

…After I called you I felt so good that I went shopping…

*I got some wooden egg cups made of native wood – I thought that perhaps
the children would eat more eggs if they had some special egg cups…*

*Then for Danny – I got a little wooden stool for sitting only – as it is
curved to fit the butt – such as the bush native children use… For Paul
– there is a whip made of rubber – with a dog's head molded at the end
and he may have it – if he promises not to hit anyone or anything with
it – not for use on Skipper.*

*…While I was in the curio shop – I saw a candelabra – with seven
holders for candles – made of brass – repaired several times but very
odd and very graceful – it was very dirty and did not look like much of
anything. I inquired about it and it is over 100 years old. I bought it
and for the last two hours I have been polishing it with liquid jewelers
rouge and it is starting to look beautiful. I thought it would make an odd
and unusual centerpiece for our table – with seven candles in it – I will
work on it for a few more days and then send it to you. Darling I hope
that you like it – and I feel sure that you will. It is a token of my love
for you.*

From Mil to Morrie

July 11, 1943

Stockton, Ca

The chicken for our picnic dinner is in the oven, all the windows are
closed, and shades drawn against the heat that is beating in already, at
10:30 a.m., the boys are outdoors, hunting "wady bugs", under which
classification come all things that crawl and creep, as far as Danny is
concerned. Paul gets so disgusted with him — he shouts he has a wady
bug and when Paul goes to see it is a sow bug, the kind that roll up into a
little ball. "Oh, that's not a lady bug, Danny, that's a salad bug."

―

From Morrie to Mil

July 18, 1943

APO687 Edinburgh Field, Trinidad

This is not the season for grasshoppers and when they do come into season
I will get several of them and send them to the boys. When I go down to
Surinam again I will purchase the box of bugs for the boys — the box itself
is beautiful with a glass inlay, under which are butterfly designs.

―

CYNTHIA LIPTON

*F*ROM ROSE TO MORRIE

August 14, 1943

Stockton, Ca

Mil told you of my plans, but now, that we are again in uncertainty about
your plans; everything seems to be jumbled again. One thing is sure, that
I won't make any move, be it Stockton, Dallas, or Chicago, until we get
the sure thing from you. It seems to be my lot to be moving and traveling
around constantly… I am very much pleased with the progress you are
making and the outlook for more to come and I hope that the change is all
for the better. I like the candelabra very much. Is it for Jewish ritual?

—

*F*ROM MIL TO MORRIE

August 15 1943

Stockton, Ca

We just got back from Jenny Loew's, where we had a very nice time
visiting with her and her cousin… We sat around and talked, talked about
Irving – Jenny's cousin took Irv's classes and says everyone loves him, that
he is the outstanding prof on campus, that they all think him somewhat of
a genius, etc. So Ma [Rose] told a few stories about Irving… A very nice
visit.

I would have loved to hear Rose tell stories of young Irving
Goleman. Rose filled the role of Irving's second mother. Though Morrie
was six years younger than Irving, the two were as close as brothers.

From Morrie to Mil

August 16, 1943

APO868 Port of Spain, Curacao, Trinidad

…I had a rather hard day today – I had to go to a camp to inspect and I spent most of the day riding in a car through coconut groves. The roads were very winding and we had to cross two rivers on a very primitive ferry that was propelled by a man pulling on a cable. One of the ferryboat men had elephantiasis of the leg – the first case I have seen. It was very interesting.

—

From Mil to Morrie

August 18, 1943

Stockton, Ca

Darling:

…My fingers are surely crossed for your leave – and crossed tighter so maybe you'll get it in December, as I would love for you to be home for Xmas. It won't be long before Paul will lose faith in Santa, and then it is a different sort of Christmas – but when they come into the living room, wide-eyed with wonder and surprise and awe – I'd hate for you to miss it again. Besides, I want you for Christmas for myself.

Mr. Devere is going to set up the gym set tomorrow morning, and I can't wait for it to get up – Paul can't walk the earth like a human these days, he is standing on his head, or walking on windowsills, or turning somersaults, or climbing trees, etc. He even climbed to the roof of a boat house in Hibbards' backyard – they are neighbors to the Deveres. It isn't a high roof, but I certainly gasped when I saw him up there...This morning Mary and her husband asked if they could take the boys out to the port [Port of Stockton] with them. We couldn't find Paul, so Dan went. I later found Paul in a tree, in Campbell's back yard.

Mary said Dan created a real bottleneck there – all work stopped so everyone could admire him and laugh at him and marvel at him. Major Feu was so taken with Dan that he held him in his lap, let him answer the phone, took him for a ride in a jeep, took him to see acres and acres of parked jeeps, took him to the fire house, took him to where there was a puppy. And just went nuts about him.

...But the boys are sweet in spite of it all. Ma [Rose] is quite pleased to find that Paul isn't so antagonistic towards her as he always seems to have been. I didn't tell her she has changed and doesn't command him to do this and that anymore. Tonight they had lots of fun together. Paul was a mouse, squeaking and hiding from her. He gave her the first real spontaneous kissing and hugging she has had since she came here. Danny more that makes up in mushiness what Paul doesn't give her – he is constantly mushing with _his_ grandma.

FROM MORRIE TO MIL

August 18, 1943

APO868 Port of Spain, Curacao, Trinidad

...First off – I bought a radio – a Hallicrafter for $100.00. It plays very well and I like it. I may have overpaid a bit for it but I know I can turn around and get $150.00 for it right now... Nice that Irv and Fay and the kids came over – too bad that you and Fay do not attract each other but Fay is really a funny duck and I don't blame you if you are not too fond of her.

—

FROM MIL TO MORRIE

September 9, 1943

Stockton, Ca

Hello, Darling:

As I sat listening to the 10 o'clock news, I wondered if November 11th is going to be as eventful a day this year as it was 25 years ago. I also wonder if, after the European war is over, you will see service under Stilwell again? Time alone will tell. However, it looks more and more like after your two years overseas time are up, you might be coming home to stay, please God – please.

...Franz and Clara stopped in for a little while tonight, after dinner, and Clara asked me if I thought Rudy should be out of gowns and into pants already. He is not quite eight weeks old. So she and Franz proceeded to

have quite a discussion about how to dress a child. Franz wants her to raise him like a poor man's son, and thinks she should study and copy the Mexicans in their child-raising. I tell you, they are so funny, but I don't dare to laugh as they are in earnest about it all.

...Franz is very happy about the Italian situation, as his mother is in Genoa, you know. However, in tonight's report, Genoa is still in German hands and is in fact being reinforced by them. Guess they'll not hold it long though.

—

FROM MORRIE TO MIL

September 10, 1943

APO868 Port of Spain, Curacao, Trinidad

...the censorship regulations have been reinterpreted and all I can mention is somewhere in the Caribbean. So do not mention the places in your letters either. ...The Russians are doing very well and so are the British and Americans. The capitulation of Italy gives me new hope for an early end to this war... This will mean that there will be a shuttle from Italy to England over Germany and back – dropping a load of bombs on each trip over Germany. Good, say I. I hope Germany gets pulverized. This is the first time in 100 years that that dastardly aggressive nation has had the war brought home to her own territory, and perhaps she will think twice before she starts another war.

—

From MORRIE TO MIL

September 24, 1943

APO868 Port of Spain, Curacao, Trinidad

Dearest Mil:

I cannot understand why you have not gotten my letters saying it is alright for you to move… What are you going to do when you get to Chicago – stay with your mother and look for an apartment or house? …I hope that you will be able to find someone to go with you to Chicago… Have you considered the possibility of going by air? It would take a total of about 10 hours as contrasted to 60 by train – the only objection to that as I see it is that you might not get priorities on the plane and even if you do, you would have no assurance that you would not be taken off somewhere en route to make place for a more important passenger.

From MIL TO MORRIE

October 1, 1943

From the train enroute from Stockton to Chicago

This will have to be the merest note as the train is rocking so. However, just to let you know we are really on our way. Nearly all of Stockton came down to the station to see us off… I had another of my headaches yesterday, but a good one. Woke up with it and wanted to do so much but couldn't. Got the important things done and got out to Fay's, where *all had gone well in my absence. The Goleman children are delighted with the birds. Irv set up one bracket on their front porch and one in the children's room. At dinner time that Wilson fellow came along and he and the Goleman's got deep into a nail chewing discussion. It seems the G's have bought a lot out near the college. 8000 sq ft. They had invested all of $25 in it already. The discussion was – shall the master bedroom be upstairs or downstairs? I laughed till I cried – they were so much in earnest about how the kitchen should open on to the patio and the dining room must get most of its light from a glass wall on one side. Sounds idyllic and tremendous. Fay's house was such a mess, I asked where the servant's quarters would be for such a big house.*

—

FROM MORRIE TO MIL

October 3, 1943

APO868 Port of Spain, Curacao, Trinidad

At this time or shortly you will be in Chicago. I do hope the trip was not too tiring for you… Did Fay or Irving come over at least to get the love birds or did you have to deliver them? I gather from your letters that your social intercourse with the Golemans has been confined lately to telephone. Fay is a funny duck…Did I tell you that I love you and adore you and worship you and that you are my sweetheart and always will be? Kiss Mom [Isabella] for me. How did she like the medal?

—

FROM MIL TO MORRIE

October 3, 1943

Chicago, Ill.

*Well we got here – eight hours late, but all in one piece and not utterly
exhausted from the trip… I asked Mama if she would move with me
and she said she would… Had a wonderful welcome home from all the
relatives – Mama [Isabella] clutched me to her more than ample bosom
and called me her baby – her "filia benedita" which is something I can't
really translate but which is super-special and all the while I was leaning
over at a dangerous angle, clutched to her as I was…*

FROM MORRIE TO MIL

October 9, 1943

APO868 Port of Spain, Curacao, Trinidad

Dearest Mil:

*Today I received your first letter from Chicago. …I am very pleased
to hear that your Mom [Isabella] is going to move with you and I do
hope you find a nice adequate place near a school for the boys. Keep me
informed. Nice that you were welcomed so royally – I'll bet your mother
nearly squeeeeeeeezed you and the boys to bits. I wish that you and Paul
and Danny could do that to me. Maybe it will happen before I think it
will. I hope so.*

From Mil to Morrie

October 10, 1943

Chicago, Ill.

Paul is such a wonderful boy; I feel we can't give him too much. That Danny boy is a charmer and a politician; he'll get what he wants by himself. Paul is going to have to work harder for his things.

—

From Morrie to Mil

October 13, 1943

APO868 Port of Spain, Curacao, Trinidad

Nice that so many people came to see you off. Glad that the Goleman children enjoyed the birds so much. I know they will have much pleasure from them. Did Paul or Danny object to your giving them away?

—

From Mil to Morrie

October 13, 1943

Chicago, Ill.

Hello my Darling:

Again I say, "wot a day, wot a day" I dreamed of peace and quiet and late sleeping and lots of reading. I certainly was nuts. Woke up to find it still raining… Stayed home and Mom and I worked… to get the stuff cleared out of the living and dining rooms. She said she would put stuff in the basement. Now it comes time to put it there and she starts demurring, "It gets so musty smelling in the basement, maybe I can squeeze it in some place up here." So, I let her struggle with dimensions — after all, only so much can be squeezed into one dresser and that's that. Meanwhile, I started clearing out the other rooms. A friend of Vi's who thought she was in labor came knocking on the door. It is her second child, full term, but she had a backache, no spotting, her pains were very irregular as she didn't know whether to go to the hospital or not. As she had had these pains for just a couple of hours I advised her to wait a bit. About an hour and a half later, her husband (whom I had never met before, came tearing in the house, "Will you come cut the cord, the baby's here!" So I flew over and we were both so excited and running pell mell, tumble bumble, that our neighbor screamed, "What's the matter?" We didn't stop to answer. The baby was yelling, the girl's mother was standing by wringing her hands and everything was wild. The cord was still pulsating. In no time at all, the doctor came so he did the rest and I just stood by and helped. I straightened her out and then oil bathed the baby, a beautiful little fat pink girl.

—

FROM MIL TO MORRIE

October 10, 1943

Chicago, Ill.

…We are all well here, though Paul was in a tearful, somber mood when he went to bed. He insists on having Aesop's Fables read to him and I hate them because almost all have such unhappy endings, which might *portray life more realistically, but which are hard on such a sensitive one. It happened when I read about the Stag and the Wolf. Seems the stag admired his antlers, but despised his thin legs. A wolf gave him chase and his legs served him well, but his beautiful antlers got him caught and the wolf devoured him …suddenly Paul buried his face in my arm and sobbed that he didn't want the deer to be killed.*

—

*F*ROM MORRIE TO MIL

October 15, 1943

From Wing Hq. Air Command APO868 c/o P.M.N.Y

Dearest Mil:

Hope we will be together when our 10 grandchildren gather around to honor us on our birthdays or wedding anniversary. Darling I love you so very much.

Lipton family ca. 1943. Left to right: Mil, Danny, Paul, and Morrie, a flight surgeon in the Army Air Corps, Stockton Field.

Paul Lipton and Deborah Goleman ca. 1943, Stockton, CA

*Danny Lipton with the
Goleman girls—Deborah and
Judith.*

Silver Lake 1949

Mil and Rose with the Lipton boys. Left to right: David, Paul, and Danny.

Deborah Goleman 1944.

Judith Goleman 1944.

Lipton family portrait ca. 1950. Dan is grimacing, Paul is grinning, and David is looking forlorn and cute..

Rose Lipton with Paul in the Indian costume and Danny in the stroller.

Man in the Mid-20th Century. Debrah and Judith Goleman with their little brother, Danny Goleman ca. 1950.

Dr. Morris Lester Lipton, my dear Grandpa.

Mildred Formento Lipton my sweet Grandma.

Thi is the way I remember Morrie and Mil. Antioch, CA 1960s.

Rose Lipton at the La Brea Tar Pits in Los Angeles, CA, 1950s.

CHAPTER 14

SCORCHED EARTH AND THE
CITY OF LAHORE

———

I am intrigued by the following passage that Morrie wrote to Irving in
that letter from March, 1943:

> Glad that your mother [Ida Goldman] *managed to ship Aunt Bertha*
>
> [Bertha Levin] *away because I really think that she is a vixen.*

My grandfather Morrie was a firstborn male, as is my father, my
brother, my husband, and my son. I've wondered about the significance
of this position in the birth order. I am sure I see some similarity of
confidence, entitlement and achievement among the firstborn men in my
life. After all, they each had their mother's undiluted attention during the
early first part of their lives.

I heard once that a high percentage of astronauts are either firstborn
or only children. Undiluted mother love makes you believe you can reach
beyond the atmosphere. The younger children, like Herman and Bertha,
and my own daughter Carolyn are swept into the flow.

So the seven Lipstein siblings are arranged like this: Ida, Fannie, Goldie, Herman, Bertha, Anna, Della. Aunt Bertha fascinates me. Morrie calls her a vixen and he was happy she had been shipped away by Ida Goldman. Why? I can discover and imagine Bertha through some of her early travels.

Reel back to the first visit Aunt Bertha made to Rose and Herman. In 1913, Bertha Levin traveled with her two children, Manuel, age eight, and Gloria, age six. The SS Oceanic set sail from Southampton on December 26, 1912.

The magic of ship travel for children at this time is brought to life for me in a poem by Rudyard Kipling. It is called "Fifty North by Forty West" and was first published in *St. Nicholas Magazine*, December 1897.

I have always loved Mowgli, and the *Jungle Books*, but I love the *Just So Stories* most, like *The Cat Who Walked by Himself* and *How the Whale Got His Throat*. When they were little, my own kids, one or both, would climb up to the upper bunk. I'd be on the bunk below, curled up on my back, sticking my feet up through the slats, pushing and rocking the mattress in a rollicking motion as I recited that Kipling poem. Bumping and booming, the kids squealed as they were tossed about:

> *When the cabin port holes are dark and green,*
> *Because of the seas outside,*
> *And the ship goes wop with a wiggle between,*
> *And the steward falls in the soup tureen,*
> *And the trunks begin to slide,*

When Nursey lies on the floor in a heap,

And Mummy tell you to let her sleep [Let Me Sleep!]

And you aren't waked or washed or dressed,

Then you'll know, if you haven't guessed,

You're Fifty North and Forty West.

After a long sea voyage, on January 3rd, 1913, my great aunt Bertha and the kids, Manuel and Gloria, got off the boat in New York Harbor. They were on their way to the Varsity Theater in Champaign, Illinois.

Herman had convinced his sister Bertha and her husband Julius Levin to get into moving pictures, to open the first moving picture house, a Bioscope, in Cape Town, South Africa. And so the Levins came to see the Varsity Theater and how it was run. Herman Lipstein and Julius Levin were early cinema impresarios. Jews were at the groundswell of the burgeoning movie industry. After checking out the Varsity, the Levin's moved to South Africa and established the movie business in Cape Town.

Between the years 1880 and 1910, the Jewish population in Cape Town grew from 4,000 to 40,000. The influx of Yiddish speaking immigrants from Lithuania expanded the Jewish community so much that Cape Town became known as a Lithuanian colony.

Aunt Bertha, Uncle Julius and the children landed in South Africa after the Second Boer War, but before the Great War. I see them as adventurers, impresarios, fortune-seekers, entrepreneurs.

South Africa, at that time, was a place where the earth was still scorched by British Imperialism. The Boers had won the First Boer War, but that was all erased when the British won the Second Boer War.

The Boers in South Africa were descended from immigrants who sought religious freedom. Throughout the years, pioneers known as Voortrekkers made the Great Trek into the interior from the Cape Colony. The Voortrekkers founded two independent republics, the Orange Free State and the Transvaal Republic.

Then, in 1886, gold was discovered in the Transvaal and by 1899, British forces were gathering on the borders of the Boer Republics of the Orange Free State and the Transvaal.

The Boers attacked first. This strike against the British started the Second Boer War in 1899. The British suffered extensive losses for underestimating the marksmanship, horsemanship and guerilla techniques of the Boer commandoes. South African Jews fought on both sides of the conflict.

My dearly beloved storybook author, Rudyard Kipling was a Nobel Laureate and the Bard of British Imperialism. He wrote the poem Ubique about the Second Boer War.

Ubique Royal Artillery

There is a word you often see, pronounce it as you may--
"You bike" - "you bykwee" - "ubbikwe"--alludin' to R.A.
It serves 'Orse, Field, an' Garrison as motto for a crest;
An' when you've found out all it means I'll tell you 'alf the rest.

Ubique means the long-range Krupp be'ind the low-range 'ill--

Ubique means you'll pick it up an', while you do, stand still.

Ubique means you've caught the flash an' timed it by the sound.

Ubique means five gunners' 'ash before you've loosed a round.

Ubique means Blue Fuse, an' make the 'ole to sink the trail.

Ubique means stand up an' take the Mauser's 'alf-mile 'ail.

Ubique means the crazy team not God nor man can 'old.

Ubique means that 'orse's scream which turns your innards cold!

Ubique means "Bank, 'Olborn, Bank - a penny all the way" -

The soothin', jingle-bump-an'-clank from day to peaceful day.

Ubique means "They've caught De Wet, an' now we shan't be long."

Ubique means "I much regret, the beggar's goin' strong!"

Ubique means the tearin' drift where, breech-blocks jammed with mud,

The khaki muzzles duck an' lift across the khaki flood.

Ubique means the dancing plain that changes rocks to Boers.

Ubique means mirage again an' shellin' all outdoors.

Ubique means "Entrain at once for Grootdefeatfontein."

Ubique means "Off-load your guns" - at midnight in the rain!

Ubique means "More mounted men. Return all guns to store."

Ubique means the R.A.M.R. Infantillery Corps.

Ubique means that warnin' grunt the perished linesman knows,

When o'er 'is strung an' sufferin' front the shrapnel sprays 'is foes;

An' as their firin' dies away the 'usky whisper runs

From lips that 'aven't drunk all day: "The Guns! Thank Gawd, the Guns!"

Extreme, depressed, point-blank or short, end-first or any'ow,

From Colesberg Kop to Quagga's Poort - from Ninety-Nine till now -

By what I've 'eard the others tell an' I in spots 'ave seen,

There's nothin' this side 'Eaven or 'Ell Ubique doesn't mean!

Definitions:

Krupp: *German field gun used by the Boers*

Blue Fuse: *extreme range fuse for a bursting shell*

trail: *rear support piece of a gun-carriage*

Mauser's 'alf-mile 'ail: *the Boers were famed as long-range marksmen with their Mauser rifles.*

'Olborn, Bank: *A London omnibus line*

De Wet: *Christiaan De Wet, elusive Boer general of the guerilla phase of the war.*

drift: *ford*

Grootdefeatfontein: *Grootfontein was a site on the Groot river*

R.A.M.R.: *Royal Artillery Mounted Rifles, formed from artillery companies when mounted infantry were needed.*

shrapnel: *bursting shell fragments*

Ninety-Nine: *1899, onset of the Boer War*

Who invented the concentration camp? The British during the Second Boer War. In 1900, British Tommies captured convoys of both refugees and Boer commandoes. The Boer guerillas were interned as POWs in Sri Lanka, India, St. Helena and Bermuda.

The Boer women and children were taken to concentration camps like the one near Bloemfontein.

To see Bloemfontein, I had only to read this vivid, first-hand account of the experience of a young Boer girl named Johanna Uys:

"You'll get food, everything you need in the camp," the Tommies said. At Bloemfontein, we were placed in carts. We were taken three miles outside town and dumped down on the veld. They put up bell-tents for us, one next to the other. Hundreds of round tents, far as the eye could see.

We were issued ration cards and stood in line for food. We got meat, sugar, mealie meal, condensed milk. The sun burnt us black. Our shoes wore out. Our clothes were un-ironed and filthy. The toilet was horrible. A big hole with plank seats and sacking around it, you climbed up on top of the planks. No newspaper, no rags. The camp was lice-infested. I watched Tommies take their leggings off, unwinding them like strips of bandages. They used broken glass to scrape the lice from their legs. My aunt had to cut all my hair off. Theft was rife. There were fights between women. Prostitutes carried on with Tommies and Boers in the camp. Most of the men were elderly. One old man, called De Wet, was a bastard. He wanted to interfere with my aunt. She chased him out of the tent. Tommies also interfered with the women. My aunt became friendly with one of the Tommies. She stole someone else's skirt and walked with him. Thousands of newcomers arrived at Bloemfontein camp. Thousands became sick. The marquee hospital tents were always full. The doctors worked day and night. We found pieces of blue stone vitriol in the sugar. Lots of people were poisoned. People died like rats. Carts came down the rows of tents to pick up the dead. There were funerals every day.

Johanna (Joey) Van Uys

Emily Hobhouse was an English activist, who made a visit to Bloemfontein in 1901. She was an eyewitness and a journalist documenting the conditions in the camps. The British propaganda said the Boer children were dying from maternal neglect, but Emily Hobhouse was at Bloemfontein when 7-year-old Lizzie van Zyl died. Emily Hobhouse gives this account:

I used to see her in her bare tent lying on a tiny mattress which had been given her, trying to get air from the raised flap, gasping her life out in the heated tent. Her mother tended her. I got some friends in town to make a little muslin cap to keep the flies from her bare head. I was arranging to get a cart made to draw her into the air in the cooler hours, but before wood could be procured, the cold nights came on and she died. I found nothing to show neglect on the mother's part.

Emily Hobhouse said that it was all "a gigantic and grievous blunder, caused not by uncaring women, but crass male ignorance, helplessness and muddling. I rub as much salt into the sore places in their minds… because it is good for them…" ★

★ Anglo Boer War Museum.

Emily Hobhouse died on June 8, 1926. Her ashes are secure in a niche at the Women's Memorial at Bloemfontein.

By the time the Levins made another journey to the United States in 1918, the whole world had changed. Cape Town had changed. The Spanish Influenza and the Cape Town Musician's Strike had put them out of business. Bioscopes were shuttered to prevent the spread of the disease.

The voyage of the S.S. City of Lahore originated in Calcutta on July 31, 1918. After a stop in Durban, the ship sailed to Cape Town to pick up my great Aunt Bertha, the vixen, and her whole family. Then, the S.S. City of Lahore set course for New York Harbor. The passenger manifest reveals the assortment of travelers that began to board.

Aunt Bertha looked over her shoulder at Agnes Killer.

"Julius, you know that witch from Nova Scotia was caring for lepers in the Congo. Warn the children not to touch her."

"Bertha, she's an old missionary woman, weary and traveling home."

"Just the same, I don't want them close to her."

The old woman, named Agnes Killer, had been a missionary in the Belgian Congo. Agnes shuffled past the Levins, hunched over from the weight of the heavy cross she wore. The woman's skin was sallow and she had a tremendous hairy mole on her right eye. Her left hand was wrapped in a musty bandage and she smelled like mothballs and mildew. Agnes Killer was only 59-years-old, but her posture and complexion made her look older. This old woman had been born in Truro, Nova Scotia in 1858, the same year the railway opened between Truro and Halifax.

Since Bertha and Julius were in the moving picture business, Bertha also felt wary and suspicious of the Vaudevillians. The Vaudeville stars of the time felt threatened by moving pictures, and by the flickering sweethearts of the nascent silver screen. At that time, the flickering shadows were still silent; it seemed the flesh and blood actors could trump that with their voices, singing and speaking to the audience.

Gloria, Manuel and little Albert Levin wandered the ship, checking out the Vaudeville artists, hoping to find some playmates among the children. As the Levin kids settled in for the journey, they watched the Vaudeville artists disappear into cabins along the way.

The Vaudevillians were connected with the ATT, the Africa Theatres Trust of South Africa. And they were a raucous assortment. Clive Boyce, a 31-year-old English guy from Australia had a large scar on his left thigh. Clive's stated purpose for travel was to "tour theatrically with performing dogs." As Clive entered his cabin, the Levin kids heard the dogs yelping from crates that were loaded into the storage hold.

The Levin kids watched the Vaudevillians walk by. Next came the Dutch Kiwis, named the Wielaerts. The family stood out for their fair hair and skin. The father, Johan was a green-eyed Dutchman from Amsterdam. He squinted behind spectacles, but his vision was still weak. Johan and Catherine had met in New Zealand. Their blue-eyed boy, Tristan, was born in Auckland.

Gloria, Manuel and Albert watched with hopeful expressions as 10-year-old Tristan followed his parents to their cabin. Maybe Tristan would be good fun, as they all embarked on this next adventure to New York City.

After the Vaudevillians were settled, the Levin kids noticed a group of young men were headed to the States to study at the University of Michigan, Ann Arbor. One guy was called Redvers Merry, an Englishman, 18 years old with a burn on his right arm.

Three Boers from O.F.S., Orange Free State, were bound for the University in Michigan. Heinrich Theunissen was 22; he came from Wanderer's View, Johannesburg, and had a long scar behind his head. The second was Frans Van Reenan, a Bruin Afrikaners, so tall he towered over all the others, 23-years-old, six-foot-two, with a dark complexion. He was a farmer and a student.

The youngest of the three Boers was Dan De Wet, just over 18-years-old with a sallow complexion, blond hair, and green eyes.

Was this young man related to General Christiaan Rudolph de Wet, the elusive Boer guerilla commando that Kipling sang about in his poem, "Ubique"? Kipling said:

Ubique means "They've caught De Wet, an' now we shan't be long." Ubique means "I much regret, the beggar's goin' strong!"

The Anglo Boer War Museum has published the following passage about General Christiaan Rudolph de Wet:

During March 1902 he operated in the western Free State, but the end was in sight. The scorched earth policy and the plight of the women and children in the concentration camps brought the Boers to the negotiation table. Although De Wet was still prepared to carry on with the relentless struggle, it was clear that

most of the delegates at Vereeniging were opposed to prolonging the war. De Wet

signed the peace treaty in his capacity as acting president of the Free State

(29-31 May 1902)...He then visited the commandos to persuade them to lay

down their arms.

Names and threads connect grandfathers to grandsons, Aunt Bertha to her sister Ida, to her brother Herman, to her nephews Morrie and Irving, and to all the offspring that came after. Names and threads connect places of birth, places of travel, and places of death. Histories are interlaced, even when scholars try to parse the threads and separate the strands by neat straight lines like the history of a geographical region, or the history of a tribe of people. We are all wound together in an immense ball of yarn, like the S.S. City of Lahore, later to be rolled out and scattered for various destinations.

The Levins listed their final destination as the home of Mrs. Eva Katz, 3843 W. 18th Street, Chicago, Illinois. Bertha and her family made their way to Della's mother-in-law's home in Chicago. Aunt Della, her married name Katz was the youngest Lipstein sister.

The S.S. City of Lahore arrived in New York on November 3, 1918. The Levins came home to the United States during the deep in-breath of German surrender. That breath was let out at the 11th hour of the 11th day of the 11th month. I can imagine Bertha and Julius Levin, Della and Morris Katz, Rose and Herman Lipstein along with sisters and children, celebrating the Armistice in Chicago in 1918.

Jennie died, the Varsity burned, the Great War ended, and Herman died. As a young man, Morrie had a job in the Sear's warehouse in Chicago as a stock boy. I guess it was a pretty big place and he'd wear roller skates to get around the huge warehouse, stocking and unloading shelves. Later in life, Morrie bragged about how he had legs of iron during that time.

Prohibition was in full force when my grandfather Morrie became a pharmacist. I've heard stories that Morrie's assignment at Walgreens was to take one bottle of whiskey and turn it into two, by dilution.

The stock market crashed and the Great Depression made way for the New Deal. Hitler annexed Austria, and then came the Night of Broken Glass, with government-sanctioned pogroms against the Jews. Germany invaded Poland and World War II began in Europe. Pearl Harbor was attacked on December 7, 1941. The United States joined the war and my grandfather Morrie served in the Caribbean.

The Enola Gay and the Bocks Car dropped atomic bombs on Hiroshima and Nagasaki, and Japan surrendered. My grandfather rejoined his wife and three young sons after he mustered out of the Army at Camp Stoneman in Pittsburg, California.

CHAPTER 15

THE PITTSBURG – ANTIOCH HIGHWAY

My present job is on the site of the former Camp Stoneman. Camp Stoneman was a major staging area for the U.S. Army. At its height, it covered 2,500-acres near the town of Pittsburg, California. Camp Stoneman opened in 1942 and was the embarkation point for more than one million American soldiers headed for the Pacific during World War II.

At the close of World War II, Camp Stoneman became a separation center. Before the troops were ferried back, they had their first welcome at Fort Mason in San Francisco, with music and fanfare and entertainment and hundreds of waving, welcoming Americans. From Fort Mason, the troops boarded the ferry for the three-hour run through the bay and up the Sacramento-San Joaquin river to Pittsburg. A huge welcoming sign installed on Angel Island said "Welcome Home - Well Done."

As the Ferry crossed San Pablo Bay into the narrow Carquinez Straits, another sign hung on the C&H Sugar Refinery at Crockett. My house looks out over the waterway that those ferries traveled.

After passing Crockett, the troops could see another sign on the Benicia-Martinez Railroad Bridge. Then they moved through Suisun Bay, past Port Chicago, on to the Pittsburg docks that were decorated and festooned with ribbons.

My grandfather, Morrie, mustered out of the Army at Camp Stoneman in Pittsburg. The family, Morrie, Mil and their three sons, Paul, Dan, and David spent the first year in Pittsburg before settling in Antioch, California. Antioch was the place where the white folks settled after World War II. Pittsburg was where the black folks settled.

Just over the hill to the west, was Port Chicago. In 1942, it was called the Port Chicago Naval Magazine. Ammunition destined for the Pacific Theater was delivered to the Port Chicago facility by train, and then loaded onto cargo ships for transport to the war. The munitions included bombs, shells, torpedoes and naval mines. All the enlisted men working as loaders at Port Chicago were black. All their commanding officers were white.

The men held speed races to see who could load the munitions on the ships the fastest. On July 17, 1944, the prize for speed was an explosion that took the lives of 320 servicemen, 390 others were injured. Two-hundred-two of the dead were black enlisted men.

On that day, five thousand tons of munitions detonated. The men that survived the 3.4 Richter blast were ordered to clean up the remains of their lost comrades, with no bereavement leave or time to rest.

Then the black men were ordered to resume the munitions loading at high speed. Fifty men refused to work. These men were tried for mutiny and became known as the Port Chicago 50. They were convicted by Court Martial.

The Chief Counsel for the NAACP, Thurgood Marshall, came to observe the trial. The Port Chicago 50 were sentenced to time in prison. Marshall, who later argued in Brown v. Board of Education against "Separate but Equal" and became the first black Supreme Court Justice, declared the proceedings "one of the worst frame-ups we have come across."

On December 23, 1999, Freddie Meeks, one of the survivors of this tragedy was granted a full pardon by President Bill Clinton.

My Uncle David is the youngest Lipton son, born on December 23, 1944, during the Battle of the Bulge. David told me that he remembered a bar across from Hazel's Drive-In on the road between white Antioch and black Pittsburg, called Knapps Kozy Korner (KKK), a not-so-subtle reminder of the racial sentiment of the time.

Post-war Antioch was shiny, white and prosperous. My dad and my uncles grew up there in a "Beaver Cleaver" kind of world. The Liptons in Antioch were the quintessential family of the Late Forties, Early Fifties. I imagine boys with BB guns, bullies with firecrackers on the Fourth of July. There must have been bloody rubber-band battles and lumps of coal left in the Christmas stockings of the naughty children. But the nice children could ask Santa for whatever they wanted.

In 1946, Paul was seven years old, Danny was five years old, and David was a two-year old toddler. Morrie was home from the war and made the following lists of what Paul and Danny wanted for Christmas, 1946.

Paul's List:	Danny's List:
7 League Boots	*7 League Boots*
1 Bunny	*1 Bunny*
1 Pony	*Wheelbarrow full of*
Pet squirrel	*pumpkins*
Telescope	*1 Arabian Horse*
Chest with lock for 2 people	*Saddle*
Automatic spider	*Magic wand*
Cap gun and caps	*Cap gun with caps*
Alarm clock that: a)Rings,	*Oldsmobile for Daddy*
b)Gongs c)Throws rocks	*Watergun*
Wooden air plane	*Automatic car*

My grandmother Mil held onto various hilarious keepsakes, including this letter Uncle Dan received in 1949, when he was about age 7. It was from a friend who had moved away:

𝒻ROM MICHAEL Y. TO DANNY LIPTON

> *March 9, 1949*
>
> *Who is taking my place? My father has a ranch and if you come here it won't look like a ranch but my father calls it a ranch. And my father bought a few little lots and a couple of houses so we can rent them to other people. You know, Danny some people say that Superman is a true man but he isn't because if he was we would see him in the air so if you ever believe it's true, forget it because it isn't true so DO NOT let people talk you into it... My grandpa came over and he gave me a dollar bill.*
> *Michael Y.*

Paul and Danny visited Grandma Rose Lipton in Los Angeles and wrote letters home in awkward cursive handwriting. From the way the letters are written, in precise form, with proper grammar and spelling, I can imagine Rose Lipton sitting at a table with her two young grandsons. She was the firm task mistress, coercing them to focus and to compose letters that were both informative and correct. It takes patience to cultivate excellence in achievement, just as she had cultivated excellence in her two sons, Morrie and Al.

𝒻ROM PAUL LIPTON TO MIL AND MORRIE

> *June 11, 1951*
>
> *1752 ½ South La Brea Avenue, Los Angeles, Calif.*
>
> *Dear Dad and Mom,*
>
> *We are having a wonderful time and wish you were here. We arrived*

*Saturday. The next day we went to the beach and swam for about 45
minutes. Then we went on several rides and went home. Today we plan
to go to the Tar Pits and then on to Farmer's Market. We may get to go
to the Planetarium tomorrow or the next day. We miss you very much
and hope you will send us a letter.*

Lovingly yours,

Paul

—

FROM DANNY LIPTON TO MIL AND MORRIE

Same trip - Los Angeles, Cal.

Dear Mom and Dad,

*We are having a wonderful time. We are going to Farmer's Market today.
We went to the beach yesterday, and went swimming. Paul and I went
way out, at first I was scared. I went on the roller coaster there. Tomorrow
we are going to the beach. I got David a bank. Are you sure you don't
want anything? Yesterday at the beach I was occasionally eating.*

With Love,

Danny

It's easy to get Uncle Dan talking about what he remembers from
when he was a kid, "My father liked big time pro wrestling and I used
to go with him to the matches. He was the ring doctor and I remember
going to see someone like Rocky Brown vs. Hombre Montana."

"Where was that held?

"…at the Fairgrounds in Antioch on 10th Street. My father had to

sit ringside because he was the official ring doctor. I remember he made
me move back a few rows from ringside because I was crazy. I got too
riled up by the action."

"How old were you?"

"I don't know, around 12, I guess. One time I watched my father
go into the ring and try to pop one of the wrestler's shoulders back
in. This guy was so big and brawny and muscle- bound, my father
was huffing and puffing, but he didn't have the strength to relocate the
shoulder. The wrestler was lying on the mat and his arm was almost as tall
as my father. I think it was Leo Nomellini or one of the Sharpe brothers.
He ended up going to the hospital.

"Sometimes my father would patch up the bloody lips and eyes. He
really enjoyed it. A few years later a newspaper article showed up in the
Chronicle about a lawsuit involving Hombre Montana getting injured by
a loose board outside a restaurant somewhere at Fisherman's Wharf."

"Did the article call him Hombre Montana?"

"Yeah, it did. It said he was suing the restaurant. It also gave his
real name. Turns out that Hombre Montana's real name was Sidney
Finkelstein."

Uncle Dan told me more stories. "Sometimes Paul and I would go
up to Reno or Stateline with my father and since we couldn't go into the
casinos, we'd have to wait outside in the snow while he gambled for hours
and hours. Once he got started, he was a degenerate gambler."

"What do you remember about your Grandmother Rose?"

"We'd go down and visit her in L.A. every summer and sometimes we'd stay for two weeks. She knew that neighborhood like the back of her hand. We'd get on the bus and go to the Farmer's Market, Santa Monica pier and the beach, and the Tar Pits."

"Did she drive?"

"I don't remember her ever driving. She cooked Eastern European stuff like breaded veal cutlets and she made the best scrambled eggs. They were wonderful. I remember she'd have to get every last drop out of the egg and she'd comment on how wasteful people were nowadays. She was grouchy, but lovable.

"So was my mother. Rose and my mother didn't get along very well. One time Rose came to visit in Antioch when we lived in the house on Shady Lane. They were bitching and fighting until my father must have said something to both of them, because they both shut up. The fighting just ceased.

"I'll never forget, when Grandma Rose was leaving, she looked at my mother and said, '...and your toilet seat pinches.' That's all she could come up with to express her bottled up frustration."

"What else do you remember?"

"My father used to get together with his Jewish friends and they'd tell jokes in Yiddish and they'd be howling and crying with laughter, so I asked my father to tell me the jokes. He told me they don't translate, and I said 'Try me.' So my father told me the joke in English and he was right, they don't translate.

"I remember when your father Paul and I killed a small feral pig on Winter Island. We brought it back in our boat, and Louis Pigati, Theresa's father, butchered and dressed it for us. I'll never forget what Louis said. 'That's a pretty advanced pig for being wild. It somehow got itself castrated.'"

I asked my dad about the pig incident on Winter Island.

"Dan and I were both still living at home when we went hunting for wild pigs on Winter Island. Dan had a shotgun. I think I had a .22. Winter Island is just Tule reeds and wetlands below where the Sacramento and the San Joaquin rivers split. You had to get there by boat. I wonder whose boat we used? I remember the pigs were filthy, full of lice and muck. We did kill a little one and brought it back."

"Grandpa Pigati butchered it?"

"That's right. He did."

"Did you eat it?"

"No. That meat sat in Louis' freezer for a long time. No one ate it."

My grandmother, Mil, kept letters my dad wrote home from college.

FROM PAUL LIPTON TO MIL

> *May 6, 1957*
>
> *Carnegie Institute of Technology, Pittsburgh, Pa.*
>
> *Dear Mom,*
>
> *Just a short note to let you know I am ok, and that things are looking pretty good here. I got my Physics test back with a "C" and I think I did*

well on the Chem and History tests also. I have a date with a nurse for Spring Carnival. I've taken her out several times before and something just might develop (heh! heh!) The Delts go off social probation at midnight tonight, so there's much joy in the air. The hats we will wear at Carnival look something like safari type pith helmets. Our booth consists of a circular trough (representing the Suez Canal) with floating beer bottles in it (the ships). Slingshots are provided (the guns) and you win a pin if you block the canal by sinking a ship. The pins say: I'm an ASS er (Nasser). Good fun, eh?

Love, Paul

From Paul Lipton to Mil

May, 1957

Carnegie Tech

Hi,

I found out my Chem and History grades a few days ago: a "B" in History and a "C" in Chem. I'm shaping right up. I may even be able to stay here. I have been assured of a room in the house next semester which will help my studying a lot.

We had a great time over Carnival. I was captain of the plank jousting team – we lost but we sure as hell had a lot of fun. My date screwed me up – she had to work over most of carnival, so I was pretty plastered most of the time.

...I ought to be home in about 3 ½ weeks. Our finals start on the 29th

of this month, so it may be even sooner than that if I get a good final

schedule.

Do you know if Gail Wilson is married? If so, to whom?

Not much else to report here so I'll say goodbye. I talked to the dean and

he says I'll be able to come back here next year for sure.

Love, Paul

Then my dad dropped out of Carnegie Tech and came back to California. Paul and Theresa resumed their friendship full force, and some time in 1959, I guess mid-year, my mom got pregnant. My parents got married and they moved back to Pittsburgh, Pennsylvania, so my dad could finish school.

Theresa gave birth to the baby on March 12, 1960, all alone, and in secret. So many years later, in the days and weeks after I found out about my secret sister, it was hard for me to absorb the details of the incident. My mother may have written me, but I can't find it now if it was written down, or maybe she just told me. Anyhow, this is how I remember her account.

Mom told me that she was all alone in the hospital that day. My dad was at school, so she labored on her own until they knocked her out. The adoption had all been arranged through the lawyer and the Jewish Adoption Agency, but the hospital still made my mom carry the baby out of the facility. The newborn was swaddled and its head was covered with the blanket. My mom said she had to get in the back of a cab and hand the bundle off to the lawyer. Before she did, Theresa sneaked a small peek under the blanket and saw a shock of thick dark hair. My mom didn't know if the baby was a boy or a girl until some time later, when a paper came to their address in Pittsburgh, Pennsylvania that said, 'Lipton – girl.' She hid that paper for years under the lining in her jewelry box. She told me she was afraid my dad would make her throw it away.

When my parents came back to California from Pennsylvania, they lived in Berkeley, and my brother Thomas Michael Lipton was born. Only 18 months had passed since the first baby had been given away in Pittsburgh.

My grandpa Morrie delivered Tom. Morrie also delivered me at the old Antioch hospital, just 18 months after Tom. In the family album there's a newspaper clipping from the Antioch Ledger announcing that my birth really made news. It said I was the first girl born on the Lipton side of the family in 56 years. That was a lie.

My memories of my grandparents Mil and Morrie Lipton in Antioch are loose scraps of thoughts and pictures. I remember Grandpa Lipton took us to Disneyland, and to the Circus, and to the Icecapades, and to the Ballet.

I can see the black recliner where my grandpa sat in his pajamas. I remember when we would go to see the Christmas tree at The City of Paris in San Francisco. Sometimes we'd eat at the Hickory Pit, where Grandma would give me the paper coaster from under her coffee cup. It had a scalloped edge and a fat little pig embossed on it.

I remember Grandma Lipton reading Dr. Seuss books to us on the couch at her house, where she sat smack in the middle, on the crack between cushions, because my brother Tom and I wanted her in the middle. One of our favorite Seuss books was "Green Eggs and Ham." I remember how, one time, she made green eggs and bacon to go with the story, but I was unconvinced by the substitution of the bacon for the ham.

Every time I dry between my toes, I think about my Grandma Lipton, because she told me once, when I was little, how important it is to do that. In the bathroom of her house in Antioch, two mirrors somehow faced each other and threw an endless tunneling regression, reflection within reflection back generations through the looking glass to infinity.

I've had the rare privilege of reading Mildred Lipton's thoughts and prophesy of me:

Cindy – lovely Cindy, like yeast somehow, as irrepressible. I smile at the thought of my breathless, enchanting, 10-year-old granddaughter. I hope I don't live long enough to see her become prosaic and sedate. Life has a way of squeezing us all into some kind of mold, like so many ingots of steel pressed into the same shapes. Cindy should not have to be pressed into any shape – she's really a free form personality.

My parents, Paul and Theresa Lipton celebrated their 50th Anniversary, on August 23, 2009. The venue was the Kensington Community Center, teetering on the edge of the Berkeley Hills, just across from Blake Garden and the cloistered Carmelite Convent.

I was in charge of the invitations, and I shared custody of the RSVP list with my dad. His version was an Excel spreadsheet that he continued to re-sort and update. Mine was a paper printout with my own scratches and scrawls all over it. I'd add notes and doodles when I received acceptances and regrets.

One evening, a lady named Gail Wilson called, she was an old friend of my parents whom I can't remember ever meeting. She was very nice on the phone and offered her sincere regrets that she would not be able to attend. Some days later, I received a note from Gail. I tucked Gail's note in my pocket to read the day of the party.

On August 23, 2009, the party hall in Kensington was crowded with revelers, well-wishers and food. Lou Caputo dug into the salmon spread. Nancy Caputo assembled the industrial-sized coffee pot from miscellaneous pieces found in the cupboards. Carolyn and Sargamo arranged flowers and dressed the tables in skirts. Jack set up the multimedia-slide show.

My sister, Debbie chopped and arranged veggies and food on trays as we worked side by side in the kitchen. We yacked and joked and tried to figure out how to get the salmon spread away from Lou Caputo.

I looked up from the chopping and saw a woman standing in the doorway to the kitchen. She seemed to be waiting for a pause in the conversation. It was Jean, Norm Reynolds wife. Norm had worked for years with my father. Jean spoke my name.

"Cindy, I've been hoping to talk to you."

"Hi, Jean. It's been a long time."

"Really long. I just wanted to say I never thanked you for the pie."

"What pie?" I looked at her with a puzzled expression.

"You baked me an apple pie once, nineteen years ago, just after Bethany was born, and it was the most amazing thing. It was like pie from heaven. I just wanted to thank you for doing that. It was magical, just having the pie appear out of nowhere."

"I don't remember that. I must have lived in El Cerrito, where we had apple trees. I baked a lot of pies during that time. I guess I sent one to work with my dad to send home with Norm when your baby was born. Isn't it funny how we don't realize something small can make such an impression?"

"It was so wonderful. I really wanted to thank you for the pie."

"Thank you for telling me the story."

Soon the room quieted, the guests were settled and fed, and the feeding frenzy subsided into a noshing, snacking hum. My brother toasted our parents and I read Gail Wilson's note aloud to the gathering at the party. I spoke into the microphone.

Hi, Cindy...

As I said on the phone, I am so disappointed that I won't be able to make the party. And I apologize for being so delinquent with the RSVP, but kept thinking schedules could be worked out. However, I will be there in spirit and warm thoughts.

This is the one anecdote I can recall off-hand that might be fun:

Paul and Tom Taylor and a bunch of the "old gang" used to hang out the way kids still do, including at my home on Biglow Drive on occasion.

Once when I was away at school, Paul and Tom Taylor (at least I think Tom was with him) dropped by my folks' place in Antioch.

Dad told me the story later. He asked the guys how they were doing, and Paul said he was getting married. Dad congratulated him and asked Paul who was marrying. Your father's reply was: "A friend."

I guess Paul followed up with Theresa's name and other specifics, but my Dad was so tickled at the initial response, he said something like: "Well, I'm certainly glad you are friends!"

What a wonderful example your parents are to some of us who have not been quite as successful with marriage as they. I guess some of us forgot about marrying "friends."

And now Paul and Theresa celebrate a half-century of "friendship" and — I'm certain — so much more and deeper than even that. Or perhaps there is not anything really more profound than that for an ultimately long and happy togetherness. I hope you have a wonderful celebration. Tell your parents I will be thinking of them, and hope to see them soon.

My very best regards…

Gail Wilson

And a few days after the party I got a thank-you card from my folks. My mother was still soaring from the occasion, and overflowing with praise.

*F*ROM THERESA LIPTON TO CINDY, KENNAN, JACK, AND
CAROLYN

> *August 26, 2009*
>
> *Berkeley, Ca*
>
> *Dear Ones-*
>
> *The thank-yous and the love circle the globe – to the moon – to Pluto*
> *and back again.*
>
> *Mil and her brother Mike cornered me one day and were badgering*
> *me to tell them what I wanted my children to be. I kept my cool and*
> *answered, 'Good people.' You have fulfilled that desire beyond my wildest*
> *expectations.*
>
> *This celebration has caused us to pause and count our blessings. What has*
> *always been there overwhelmed us. It is difficult to put into words the joy*
> *we have in our family.*
>
> *Love,*
>
> *Mom and Dad*
>
> *Grandma and Grandpa*

My mother's parents, Martha and Louis Pigati.

CHAPTER 16

DUSTBOWL OKIES

One day I drove to Salinas to find the grave of John Steinbeck and to dig some of his famous dirt. I couldn't help running the lyrics of Me and Bobby McGee through my head, "Somewhere near Salinas, Lord, I let him slip away; he's looking for that home and I hope he finds it…"

Salinas looks just like the San Joaquin Delta, which looks just like the Mississippi Delta. The farmlands of Salinas give off the same hot, flat smell. The same long horizons stretch out under the same big skies that always hang over farmland.

The drive was so long I had to pull off the road at one point and find a semi-private tree to take a leak. Once again I was grateful that wilderness peeing is one of the skills in my hippie repertoire. I think I learned as a kid by peeing in a coffee can during long road trips in our VW bus, California license plate RMF 739. I finished, hiked up my pants and I was back on the road.

I found the cemetery and drove in. I had written down the plot coordinates, but found it difficult to get my bearings and figure out how the field of graves was mapped. John Steinbeck; Plot: Block N-5; Garden of Memories Memorial Park; Salinas; Monterey County; California; USA; North America; Earth; Sol Solar System; Milky Way Galaxy; Universe.

I zig-zagged and looked for plot markers. Then I happened upon a clue. It was a sign that said: "John Steinbeck's Grave" with an arrow pointing down a row of monuments.

I made my way to his family plot, and even though it is sealed with stone, I dug some dirt out of the side where John Ernst Steinbeck is buried, poured whiskey in the small hole and buried some silver dimes.

Steinbeck, a Socialist writer, was an eyewitness and a journalist who documented the plight of the migrant Okie farm workers in his book of articles about the people he called the "harvest gypsies."

The Okies were despised undesirables in California, having scattered westward in the Diaspora caused by the severe drought in the Midwest. In 1936, Steinbeck published *The Harvest Gypsies: On the Road to the Grapes of Wrath.*

At this season of the year, when California's great crops are coming into harvest, the heavy grapes, the prunes, the apples and lettuce and the rapidly maturing cotton, our highways swarm with the migrant workers, that shifting group of nomadic, poverty-stricken harvesters, driven by hunger...from crop to crop, from harvest to harvest, up and down the state...On side roads and near rivers where

there is little travel, the squalid, filthy squatters' camp will have been set up, and the
orchards will be filled with pickers and cutters and driers.

The unique nature of California agriculture requires that these migrants
exist, and that they move about. ...a large peach orchard which requires the work
of 20 men the year round will need as many as 2000 for the brief time of picking
and packing. And if the migration of the 2000 should not occur, if it should be
delayed even a week, the crop will rot and be lost.

...In the past they have been of several races, ...Chinese in the early period,
then Filipinos, Japanese and Mexicans....But in recent years the foreign migrants
have begun to organize, and at this danger signal they have been deported in great
numbers, for there was a new reservoir from which a great quantity of cheap labor
could be obtained.

The drought in the Middle West has driven the agricultural population
of Oklahoma, Nebraska, parts of Kansas and Texas westward. Their lands are
destroyed and they can never go back to them. Thousands of them are crossing the
borders in ancient rattling automobiles, destitute and hungry and homeless, ready to
accept any pay, so that they may eat and feed their children.

Some of my people were swept out of the Oklahoma dustbowl, on
to California by way of Illinois. My Grandma Pigati, my mother's mother,
Martha Henrietta Chrétien was born in 1905, during the birth pangs of
Statehood in Oklahoma, Indian Territory.

At that time, Choctaw, Cherokee, Creek, Chickasaw, Seminole,
Negro, and White people all lived in the Territory. By 1905, millions of

tons of bituminous coal had been mined out of Choctaw Nation land. Oklahoma sawmills worked elm, oak, pecan, and ash. My grandma, on my mother's side, was born among miners, farmers and cattlemen. North of the Arkansas River and east of the Neosho, streams and rivers cut into the Ozark Plateau.

Grandma Pigati was French Catholic and my mother remembers, "Mom was born in Oklahoma when it was still Indian Territory, 1905. Some of her sayings were definitely Southern. Her thinking and cooking were a little French, a little Italian and a little 'Southern.'" The Italian came from her marriage to my grandfather, Louis Pigati, who had come over from Italy as a child.

Grandma Pigati's brother, August (Gus) was lost in the Battle of Chateau-Thierry in 1918. Her mother, Therese Chrétien, was one of the Gold Star Mothers, the ladies who laid wreaths on the graves of the war dead from the Great War (World War I). My great grandmother Therese travelled to France to lay flowers on Gus's grave.

My mother was born in Spring Valley, Illinois, in the blaze of August, 1936, a fiery Leo. She was the third child of Louis and Martha Pigati.

The family moved to California when Theresa was just a baby. As Theresa got bigger, she used to tell her mom she was hungry and she'd get this answer,

"Eat one hand, save the other one for tomorrow."

"I'm gonna tell people you never feed me."

"Yeah, and they'll take one look at you and never believe a word."

My mother said her mother Martha used to sing her old Southern hymns like, "I come to the garden alone, while the dew is still on the roses."

Grandma Martha Pigati would brag, "I have an automatic dishwasher, too, I call it Theresa."

Grandma Martha and my mom would sing in the kitchen, but never at the table. Superstitions and sayings flowed from Grandma Pigati -- like eating the heel of the bread will give you big tits; like don't ever go back to the house to get something after you're on your way -- bad luck.

I have an envelope addressed to me in my Grandma Martha's handwriting. The original note or card is long gone, but I use it to keep some other small relics of remembrance from my Pigati grandparents. This is my Catholic ephemera.

I have the prayer card from Grandpa Pigati's funeral in 1976. I remember sitting in the pews at Higgin's Funeral home in Antioch and feeling nothing. I knew so little of Louis Pigati; I had shared so little with him.

I could see his face in the casket from across the room, but I chose not to approach. I saw a family friend, named Pat, go up and kneel and cross herself. Her gestures seemed out of character.

My grandmother Martha went to the side of the casket, took my grandfather's dead face between her hands and kissed him on the mouth. And my brother sat in a pew just across from me and sobbed. I was struck that my brother could feel such deep sorrow for Grandpa Pigati, but then

I remembered that they had shared time together in the garage with the tools, and maybe sometimes went fishing.

Years later, my Mom let me look through boxes of Pigati artifacts. I held Louis Pigati's wallet in my hand. I had stolen the wallets of both of my grandfathers, pick-pocketed the past to raid their secrets and keep them safe for posterity.

Louis Robert Pigati carried a Mexican leather wallet stamped with the image of a panther and an Aztec chieftain. Thick black stitches bind the edges. I turned it over in my hand and noticed that it was so worn that the impression of a coin was stamped into the leather. I could discern the Lincoln penny silhouette.

I found coupons from the Irish Sweepstakes, a lottery numbers game, printed with exotic colored portraits that held the promise of a huge money prize to the lucky winner. I found fishing licenses and a metal Social Security card that was oxidized green, number 356-03-4218.

Grandpa Pigati carried his Selective Service card from March 29 1945: "Order No. 10404 has been classified in Class 4-A."

I read Louis Pigati's WPA Form 402 – Notice to Report for Work on Project.

> You are asked to report ready for work at 7 A.M. on 1-20-37 at City
> Bldg as Laborer on project number 8156
> – Wage class, unskilled
> – Location of project Spring Valley, Illinois.

After the Pigatis had moved to California, Grandpa Pigati worked for U.S. Steel.

"My father always worked at the Steel Mill," Theresa said. In his wallet I found a laminated card that read:

United States Steel Corporation

This permanent pass, authorizing entry to Pittsburg Works, is issued for the personal use of Louis R. Pigati 7/31//67. As a retired employee, you are welcome to return and visit the plant. Please present this pass whenever you enter the plant, and sign the register at the gate of entry.

When I was a kid and we visited Grandma Pigati, we'd play rummy or Triple Yahtzee. Grandma would call you a "cheater pig" if you tried something funny. She kept score on a brown paper sack that had been folded and refolded, inside out, in so many directions, until every square inch was used up.

Aunt Mary was there sometimes and she'd give us a five dollar bill. For the New Year we would say, "Bonjour, Bon Annee, Parfait Sante" and we'd get a silver dollar from the coffee can full of winnings from the dollar slots in Reno.

Grandma Martha Pigati kept cans of Campbell's Chicken and Rice soup stashed in the linen closet in the hall and we'd have soup with mushed up Saltine crackers. When she fixed us a salami sandwich, she'd excise the black peppercorns from the meat, so it wouldn't be too spicy for us.

When we stayed over, we'd watch soap operas or Lawrence Welk, and swing in the backyard. Grandpa Louis Pigati sat in his swivel recliner, drank Schlitz beer and watched TV, his stormy Italian eyebrows stitched into a frown.

In my little envelope, I have the prayer card for my Grandmother Martha Pigati. It was embossed in a hurry, her middle initial is wrong, and her last name is misspelled. On the other side is the Infant of Prague surrounded by small angel faces in the clouds.

Grandma Pigati's funeral was just days before Christmas, 1979, and the church altar was decorated with red poinsettias. I remember holding hands with my cousin, Lori, when we walked across the street from Higgins Funeral Home to Holy Rosary Church on A Street in Antioch. We kids, my brother, my cousins and I didn't go to the cemetery that day.

Years later, I went to visit and I brought fresh flowers on my grandmother's birthday. All the other graves were decorated with plastic and silk flowers. It turned out that real flowers are not permitted in the Catholic Cemetery, except during the actual burial. I thought it was strange that Memory Gardens, just over the hill in Concord, permitted both real flowers and fake ones. In the spirit of defiance, I filled my vase with water and left the fresh flowers. I left my Grandpa Pigati a Schlitz beer instead.

Soon after Grandma Martha Pigati died, when I was a teenager, I wrote a poem for her called Grandmother's Words:

She touched me and mumbled words

She counted on me like a rosary bead,

On a silver string.

She accepted life and grumbled no words

Only love for the misfits she bore,

And their misfits in turn.

She died and left us her words

Or no words to the wise,

She let us learn by our mistakes.

White-shrouded as the priest uttered words

Light incense and tears,

And I saw myself hanging,

A tiny bead on her rosary string.

My mother was offended by the poem I had written after my grandmother's death. Maybe she felt uneasy with religious symbolism, maybe she objected to being called a misfit. So I wasn't Catholic enough to be a Catholic; I wasn't Jewish enough to be a Jew; I wasn't educated enough to be an intellectual; I wasn't cynical enough to be an Atheist and I wasn't allowed to be a misfit. While those around me were marked by their identities, I was unmarked, because I was nothing in particular. I was imprinted on these identities, of Jew, of Catholic, of Intellectual, of Atheist, but I didn't belong.

As a young woman, Theresa, my mother, wrote a college paper about Evolution. She loved science and Darwin and scorned religious creation. I have always thought of both of my parents as Atheists.

Theresa has admitted that once upon an experience, she felt the strong calling to come up to an altar and to share in the communion, but she resisted the urge. Theresa's usual gestures are to shrug off, or roll her eyes at spiritual matters, all explained away by the human desire to explain our origin and the human desire to control our fate.

In her writings, my grandmother, Mildred Lipton tells about her Damascus Road to Atheism:

Having had my nurse's training during the depression years was good too. That was before any form of health insurance so the only people in the hospital were sick ones, really sick. …Before penicillin, before any of the miracle drugs – my! People were so sick many of them died, of course. In those days people really went to the hospital to die.

That beautiful white-haired man, as powerfully built as a Rodin sculpture; he knew he would die – he wasn't afraid. That fragile old woman, like a Dresden doll, whose cancer ate through one of her hepatic veins and she hemorrhaged internally. She died with such a soft sigh – wasn't it a sigh of relief? She wasn't afraid. Her stocky husband, who lifted both clenched fists – high and wide – and ordered God to take her. He did.

Then there was that really old woman who knew she was going to die and was so afraid she clutched at everyone who came close enough, as though holding on to someone alive would replenish her own life. Fortunately, she lapsed into a coma a day before she died. Why was she so afraid? Why were so many of them afraid? That 20-year old girl with TB, whose temperature sky-rocketed. She really burned to death no matter what was tried. She wasn't afraid. She was like a flame.

As a young student nurse, no death related to me really. There was sympathy, but not empathy. Often I went rushing off to the supply closet to cry in private, in sympathy for the living, or sobbing at the waste of a human life.

I had accepted the existence of a God, a kindly Father who loved all his children. But when a baby, a beautiful one-year old died, I stormed and raved against the divine injustice. It was that more than any other single event that made an ardent atheist of me.

I believe the only reason we even care about where we came from, and where we will go in the end, is because we are aware of ourselves as individuals. This consciousness makes each human unique and makes us fear death.

In the end, the only things left are the bones and the consciousness of each discrete human. The consciousness is the sum total of a human being's thoughts, words and ideas, the life of the mind. And the only way to get eternal life is to write this shit down.

So in the end, the only thing left are bones and thoughts poured on a page, ideas preserved by the magic of language and words. This is the way I have come to know the history, geography, lives, times and desires of my ancestors.

In the end there are only bones and memories and words.

CHAPTER 17

LOS GUILICOS RIOT

———

I took another trip to Beauty Ranch to collect the grave dirt of the pioneer children. I was able to reach under the small picket fence and leave my gifts for Lily and David Greenlaw. To hide my mischief, I pretended to be taking a rest in the shade as I scratched out a small sample of dirt from each side of the little plot. I collected the dirt in two paper bags and left my payment.

When this errand was accomplished, I set off from Glen Ellen, along Highway 12 toward Santa Rosa, to visit my uncle Dan. He lived, with his dear cousin Judy Goleman, the one with the cheeks like a lovebird, at the end of a remote country road in Sebastopol. Uncle Dan is the same toddler that Mil and Morrie cherished in their letters, who had grown up and become an old man.

After bouts with colon cancer and brain cancer, diabetes and a host of other infirmities, Uncle Dan has needed some assistance with mobility. His strength has diminished and he walks with a cane or a walker to help with his shuffling steps. When he's tired, he uses a wheelchair. The whole brain radiation he received was meant to be palliative, but he has survived well beyond medical expectations and his condition seems to have been related both to his own disease and to the radiation treatment. They call it white matter disease, WMD. It's ironic that the same acronym is used for Weapons of Mass Destruction.

On my way from Glen Ellen to Sebastopol, I came upon a road sign on Highway 12 that pointed to Los Guilicos Juvenile Detention Center. I knew about this place. Fay Goleman had written a report about the riots that happened here in March and May, 1953.

Damienne Bell describes Los Guilicos and the riots in her article about California's Mexican Period:

The old Hood House was used …to entertain ex-presidents Ulysses S. Grant, William McKinley and Theodore Roosevelt. The other buildings were used as a rest home for retired Pythians. The road leading to Hood House… Pythian Road is named for them. In 1943, the California Department of Youth Authority purchased the land and the mansion to establish the Los Guilicos School for Girls. Its reputation as an upstanding and effective alternative education for wayward girls was shattered by a four-day riot in March of 1953. One night during dinner, a 14-year-old girl incited the riot, and with the help of five others, began smashing windows and furniture. Six girls went to jail, six others were sent to Napa State Hospital, and at least thirty others were injured. That night, about sixty of the remaining girls smashed more windows, tossed toilets out of windows and stole kitchen knives as they wreaked destruction. Some escaped and robbed liquor from a Kenwood grocery store. Lockdowns, tear gas the CHP and the National Guard were required to contain them. Yet, the violence continued until thirty-eight more girls were taken to jail.

Fay Goleman had been part of a special committee appointed to study the Los Guilicos School Riots.

I pulled off the main highway and drove along Los Guilicos Ranch Road past modern buildings and a sports field surrounded by tall fences and enclosed by a net. A group of young people kicked a soccer ball. I looped around once and drove back to Pythian Road that led to the Mount Hood State Park. I found the old white brick Hood Mansion, where Presidents and Pythians and delinquent girls had been housed.

I parked in the empty lot behind the Hood House and set out with my camera to document the scene. Wooden bungalow-type buildings were interconnected by breezeways. An asbestos warning sign was posted under the Pythian crest on the padlocked double doors.

The tidy grounds around the Hood House had been planted with snapdragons and allysium, but the house had seen better days. At the front of the house, a rusted fountain stood in a circular pool with no water.

Although the paint on the porch rail was peeling off, the rail framed a green door centered on the long porch. I peered through the window. A carpeted staircase with an ornate wooden rail led upstairs from the middle of the foyer.

I walked around the side of the house and I noticed some hazy rippled window glass. I walked up the handicapped ramp to get a closer look and I pushed on the door.

It gave way, opened, and I stood there knowing I would never have this opportunity again. Before I knew it, I was inside the Hood House.

The first small room had been wallpapered with tacky, mismatched, orange squares of 1960's patchwork contact paper. The pattern looked like someone had puked up ribbon, lace, trim, and bric-a-brac from the notions counter at the dime store. I peered around corners, opened drawers and closets, all the while reminding myself that I was alone.

Careful and resolute, I walked from room to room. Some wall coverings were peeled back or water-stained, but the grandeur of the light fixtures, the marble fireplaces and the thick blue velvet drapes reminded me that presidents had visited this place.

I ventured into the most impressive room, a dining hall with a carved wooden ceiling and cabinetry, and I was struck by a painting of hunting dogs that hung above the mantel. This room had a definite masculine personality.

Rolled posters about the history of the place lay on the table and easels supported poster boards describing the restoration and rehabilitation of the property.

I felt the thick carpet under my feet as I mounted the central stairway to the upper floor. A cherub's disembodied head, the size of a basketball, rested in the corner of the stairwell landing.

The upstairs looked more dilapidated than the lower floor. Exposed wall studs and floor joists, hunks of red brick, and sunken window casements amplified the deterioration that greeted me. The second floor bathroom had a claw foot tub and a couple of porcelain commodes sat disconnected and displaced in the room.

I stole two things from Hood House: a square of red floral wallpaper that was like a scrap of litter on the floor, and a small piece of brick from the window casement. I wanted the brick because I knew it was from the original construction of the building. That brick had touched the entire history of the Hood House, from presidents, to Pythians to California Youth Authority female inmates.

A Special Committee was appointed on May 14, 1953 by the California Board of Corrections to make a special survey of the conditions at Los Guilicos which resulted in the violent riots in March and May, 1953. The report from the Special Committee is archived among the Fay Goleman papers at the University of the Pacific, Stockton library.

To research Los Guilicos, I traveled Highway 12 east into the San Joaquin Delta to the University of the Pacific Library in Stockton. I was shown to the reading room for the Holt-Atherton Special Collections and filled out the form requesting Manuscript 198, Box 3 of 5. According to the rules, I left my purse in a closet outside the reading room. No ink pens were permitted. Notes had to be taken in pencil. The archivist brought me Box 3 and I opened Folder 3.

Report of Special Board of Corrections Committee

for Study of the Los Guilicos School for Girls

Santa Rosa, California to The State Board of Corrections

On March 19, May 5, May 20 and May 24, 1953 there were disturbances at the Los Guilicos School for Girls which came to the public attention. ...Public reports of the disturbances were not entirely factual. Two matters in particular were given exaggerated emphasis in the opinion of the Committee. These were the matters of racial discrimination or so-called "race riots" and homosexuality at the school. ...There were in the student body of the School, girls of Negro, Latin American, and White ancestry. Following the first disturbance, 55 girls were removed from the school and transferred to the Napa State Hospital, the Sonoma State Home, the Mendocino State Hospital, Sonoma County Juvenile Hall, and San Francisco Juvenile Hall. Twenty-three of these were Negro, 21 were white, 9 were Mexican, 1 was Filipino, and 1 was Indian. The Committee did not find that any of these girls were transferred solely because of their racial origin, nor did we learn in the course of our investigation that the conduct of any of the girls who were ringleaders in the disturbance was motivated by any justifiable belief that girls of their own racial origin had been unduly or unjustly discriminated against. The girls themselves were frank to admit that disciplinary action meted out to them and their companions was because of conduct rather than racial origin. It is true that the precipitating cause was the transfer of two Negro girls to a State Hospital, but this was because of emotional disturbance and not because they were Negroes.

Some of the newspaper stories and one magazine article which appeared shortly after the disturbances at Los Guilicos contained statements with reference to the existence of homosexual conduct at the School. The Committee explored this subject with all of the persons interviewed. It is the opinion of the Committee that this phase of the matter had been exaggerated and some of the conduct of the staff and students had been misinterpreted. It must be remembered that the students at the school are adolescent girls. It is natural for them to form "attachments". For the most part they are seeking companionship and recognition. In their personal relationships, many of them have been deprived of wholesome, normal affection. There is bound to be certain of the girls who come to Los Guilicos who have had the misfortune of contact with adults or other juveniles who have participated in homosexual activity. The Committee believes that this number of girls is very small. The Committee was also unable to find any reliable information that would indicate that at the time of the disturbances there was any homosexual conduct between Staff and students. The statement that many of the girls were driven into homosexuality after they came to the School was totally unfounded from any information uncovered by the Committee.

Underlying Causes for Unrest which Led to Disturbances: (1) tension among inmates (2) physical plant, itself (3) deficiencies in administration, and (4) inadequacies of program.

1) Tension Among Inmates:

...Great effort was put forth through administrative orders to staff to prohibit even the most normal manifestation of adolescent friendship between girls. For example: the exchange of items of clothing and jewelry met with reprisals on the part of administration and staff. Ill-advised remarks by staff members, who were not familiar in dealing with the problems of girls of the type at the school,

often caused bitter resentment which smoldered because of lack of opportunity for
discussion between the girls and staff members.

2) Physical Plant:

…The type of construction was not one normally used in State detention
facilities and there was an abundance of glass windows used in the construction.
…When the incipient cause of the disturbance of March 19 had exploded, the girls
took advantage of the great amount of glass, physical construction of the buildings
and their location to get out of hand. The security unit in the new construction
proved entirely inadequate and this heightened the desire of the girls to escape. The
flying glass increased the hysteria among staff and students and was responsible for
some personal injuries. Some of the girls were injured attempting to crawl back into
buildings after windows had been broken out.

3) Deficiencies in Administration:

…there was a woeful failure of staff members to know their fellow workers,
no direct line of communication between staff and superiors,…no adequate
interchange of information between staff members with reference to particular girls,
initiative was thwarted by administration's refusal to encourage or permit staff
members to share in administrative problems, no efforts seemed to be expended in
developing morale or loyalty or to encourage wholesome staff relationships.

4) Inadequacies in Program:

…The academic program could not challenge them; the vocational program
was uninteresting to them; and there was little opportunity for the development
of an adequate recreational program…There was no group therapy and very little
opportunity for individual treatment for girls with special needs. Classes are held in

scattered, inadequate rooms... The quality and grade of foodstuffs purchased by the school were commendable, but from the information gathered by the committee, we are of the opinion that it is often poorly prepared, untasty, and unappealing.

The Chairman of the Special Committee was Judge William B. McKesson, from the Los Angeles Juvenile Court.

FROM JUDGE MCKESSON TO FAY GOLEMAN

July 24, 1953

Dear Mrs. Goleman:

Thank you very much for your portion of the Los Guilicos report. I have noted the changes which you mention in your note of July 16th. I have today completed the editing of the complete report and forwarded the edited copy to Harold Butterfield... I am enclosing the statement which I inserted in the report on homosexuality at the School. The word "American" to which you called my attention, on page 8, was a mistake. The word should have been Mexican. Thanks for catching the error. I am deeply indebted to you for your excellent contribution to the report and for the great amount of time you spent in connection with this committee's activity. I read with interest the discussion the three of you had in Santa Rosa. The attitude reflected in the statements of the Sheriff and his deputies bore out my previous conviction that they have had no experience dealing with adolescent girls.

When the report is completed, a copy... will be sent to each member of

the Committee... I trust you will have a pleasant Summer.

Sincerely yours,

William B. McKesson

Fay Goleman, Professor Emerita, taught sociology at the University of the Pacific from 1937 to 1976, retiring with the Order of Pacific, the highest honor the University of the Pacific bestows.

At the time of her retirement in 1976, Harold S. Jacoby, Professor of Sociology, wrote an article about Fay:

Fay found it successfully possible to combine her position as wife, and - in 1938 — mother, with an active application of her training and talents in social work, both in teaching and in agency operations. Three children were born to Fay and Irving — Deborah, Judith, and Daniel — but their arrival did not occasion any significant cessation of her career activities. In terms of public recognition she was often overshadowed by her talented husband, who as the years went by became a living legend as a classroom teacher — a legend which, since his death in 1962 has been immortalized in the Irving Goleman Center at San Joaquin Delta College. But though she took great pride in being known as Irving's wife, in her quiet and competent way she built her own career and her own reputation.

In 2009, when I tried to visit the Irving Goleman Center, I learned it was under renovation, torn apart, closed up; so much for being immortalized. The Goleman Library was closed from May 30, 2008 to

August, 2010. During this time, the collection had been moved to an off-campus stopgap called Yokuts.

No wonder Irving Goleman had been rattling around in my imagination; he was displaced from his place of enshrinement. His library was gutted, stripped to the floor joists and wall studs. It would be replaced with a new, modern facility that would serve the needs of the information technology age.

With the Goleman Library decimated, Irving began walking along the tall stacks of the collective unconscious. His spirit was at loose ends when he happened upon my curious mind. I welcomed Irving. Discovering Irving helped me distill my great grandmother Rose.

Fay had not been overshadowed by Irving. She continued her difficult social work in a society where families had needed help to manage the troubles of their own children and adolescents.

Families and tribes feel at home in a collective state. In the social contract, *We the People* consent to shed our natural state and be governed by laws. When homes and families are broken and scattered, people revert to a natural state of chaos and desperation. The riots at Los Guilicos exposed the volatile potential of troubled teenagers.

My eyes were opened to adolescent violence and despair when I served as a juror on a murder trial in Superior Count in Martinez, California, in 2009.

CHAPTER 18

BONE SAFE

The Martinez courthouse is old, from the 1920's, or maybe earlier, and the ceiling is arched with an oak leaf motif in the carved woodwork. High ceilings make me feel small. And in these chambers, I became an eyewitness and a journalist documenting the trial of a young black man accused of killing another young black man, a familiar story played out in urban courtrooms from sea to shining sea.

The judge described the two counts against the defendant: murder and attempted murder. The crimes had occurred in Richmond on December 17, 2007. The defendant was 17 years old at the time. We reached our verdict on April 17, 2009.

On the first day of jury selection, the young black defendant stood to face us as we walked in, his full head of dread-locks tied back. His boyish face seemed earnest. He wore a button-up shirt, slacks and a sweater vest.

We were warned that we shouldn't linger in the back hall because we might see the defendant walking from the jail to the courthouse in belly chains. I never saw him like that. I think it would have upset me to see him shackled.

I came to know that courthouse well. One morning, I noticed a strange door on the second floor in the side hall. The door, marked 302, was locked tight, situated as it was along the corridor between some double doors on the left and a judge's chambers on the right. I saw a brass hinged mail slot in door 302 and a handwritten sign thumb-tacked just above the slot that read, "Do Not Use Slot. Goes Nowhere."

I peeked through the slot when I thought the corridor was empty, and got a glimpse of Nowhere. Then someone came around the corner and I hurried off to sit in the sunshine of the deep windowsill and waited for the bailiff to call us in.

When we, the jury, entered the courtroom, the defendant made eye contact and smiled. He was observant enough to see that some of the jurors were belly-chained by our maternal instincts.

Everyday, without fail, a woman came and sat in the courtroom gallery from the first day of jury selection until the verdict. I realized that she was defendant's family anchor. For a long time I thought she was the defendant's mother. Not until our deliberations did I understood that that woman was his grandmother, Willie Mae Cummings.

Ms. Cummings had a face with a permanent scowl, intense, cross and determined. Her arms were thick and fleshy, and she often had her arms crossed as she watched the proceedings. She was careful never to make eye contact with the jurors. She must have been warned about tainting.

Willie Mae Cummings was there the day the verdict was read. I watched her and I watched the defendant as the judge handed Madam Clerk the verdict sheets. These were the same sheets I had filled out and signed as the presiding juror.

The defendant had his hands clasped as he faced forward to listen.

"…for the count of first degree murder, we the Jury find the defendant: Not Guilty."

He heaved a sigh and held his clasped hands under his chin as he listened to the second verdict.

"…for the count of attempted murder, we the Jury find the defendant: Not Guilty"

At this suspended moment, all I could see was his head dropping in relief, his mane of lion-like dreads hanging down. My entire perception focused only on him like a pinhole of telescopic clarity. Every other thing in the room was blurred and peripheral.

When I left the courtroom, Willie Mae Cummings was sobbing. She met my gaze full on and said, "Thank you. Thank you. Thank you." She looked like she wanted to reach out for my hands, but she restrained herself and wiped her tears on the back of her pudgy hand.

During the trial, I listened all day to testimony. Afterward I went to my job to catch up for a few hours. By the time I got home, I was exhausted.

At the same time the trial was going on at the Martinez Courthouse, I had my own personal drama unfolding with my own seventeen-year-old son. I had to deal with the pending expulsion of my almost valedictorian, popular, gentle, son, Jack.

When Jack was born he said hello to the doctor. I heard it and Kennan heard it. So did the doctor and the nurse. When Jack was a little boy, less than two years old, he would talk about Mexico.

"Do you remember when I peed in the sink in Mexico?"

"No, we don't remember that."

"Before I was born, I lived in Mexico."

"Really?"

"I had a brother in Mexico, but he died."

"How did he die?"

"He ate bad food."

My white, slightly-freckled boy with reddish hair would shovel the refried beans in and tell us Mexico stories. "When I lived in Mexico, a train tipped over and fell down the hill, and then the workman came and we had to move."

Jack was born old, an old soul, a little old man in a boy's body. I have always been proud of Jack's kindness and his skill in mediating conflicts, and I've been proud of the recognition he has gotten from his teachers and peers as a person to trust and admire.

I was sad on graduation day when I turned onto Rolph Avenue in Crockett and saw the families gathering with balloons and flowers to watch their children walk the stage in the commencement ceremony at John Swett High. Our family had no tickets to the event. Jack had picked up his diploma from the office, and the diploma was already propped up on display on our mantle. It was an anticlimactic end to thirteen years of study.

Although Jack had been specifically excluded from attending the graduation by district administrators, he decided to go to the ceremony and sit in the audience. A friend had given him a single ticket. He walked right in, no problem, and went upstairs to sit in the balcony. He had his cap and gown, still in its plastic wrapper. Even though he would not be walking the stage, they still had to give him the cap and gown. After all, we had paid for it.

During the ceremony, one of the students dedicated his speech to Jack. Afterward, Jack put on his cap and gown and joined his friends outside for pictures and congratulations.

With only two months left of high school, the students in the Contemporary Music class were restless. The teacher had been fired, and a parade of ill-equipped substitutes marched in day after day to baby-sit, but not to teach.

During this class, Jack was nosing around the closets and storage areas in the music room and found a large cake-serving knife with pink frosting stuck to it. He slipped the knife in his backpack and got the stupid idea that it would be funny to simulate a slasher scene on someone practicing in one of the individual practice rooms. So he entered the small room and he turned the lights on and off. He held up the big knife and laughed.

Not funny.

Brandishing a knife is automatic expulsion.

Tears and fighting broke out when two hundred students staged a sit-in in the John Swett cafeteria and chanted, "Bring Jack Back." But in spite of all the fighting and yelling, Jack couldn't go back.

The previous summer, Jack and a gaggle of his friends, had been selected to represent his school in Nicaragua. Here is the account Jack wrote of the day he was leader:

Day 11 of the trip was finally my turn to be leader… It was the day we hiked up an active volcano, Cerro Negro. It was also a day of celebration in Leon, called La Griteria, where natives thank the Virgin Mary for saving them from having this very volcano erupt and rain ash, ruining their crops and possibly smothering them. The holiday is quite similar to Halloween, where people of all ages go to houses and say, "Quien causa tanta alegria?" This is met by the response, "La Ascension de Maria." If you haven't already run that phrase through Google translator, the question means, "Who causes all the joy?" and the response is, "The Ascension of Mary." Afterward, a song may be sung. Personally, I didn't know the words, but one of our Nicaraguan guides, Aura did, and she sang until her voice box gave out.

But let me rewind and tell you about our day. We woke up ...drove for about an hour and we arrived at the Cerro Negro. And that's exactly what it was, a huge black hill devoid of vegetation... we were constantly hit by a very powerful, cooling breeze. In fact, the breeze was so strong, it blew my hat clean off my head, and to the bottom of the mountain. Some small child is sitting at the base of Cerro Negro, wearing a John Swett football hat as I type...As we climbed, we could smell a really strong, disgusting smell, the smell of sulfur.

...Once we reached the top, ...we needed a way to get back down. Well, for me personally, this was made by sprinting down the whole side of the hill ... I lost my footing a couple of times and went into a slide, but my momentum picked me back up, almost right back into a full sprint. It was exhilarating. I wanted to go down the hill again. Unfortunately, I did not want to do the two hour hike again for the six minute descent.

...After this, we had... quite a bit of free time. Today was the first day we could depart the hostel in groups of four without a chaperone. I didn't do this because I really just wanted to wash the black rock off my body, and relax for a while...After dinner, we went from house to house saying, "Quien causa tanta alegria?" clapping as Aura sang, and pocketing the candy, laundry detergent, combs and other goodies that the people gave us.

My father was grief-stricken when I told him of the events that led to Jack's expulsion from school. It hit him really hard, and I can't help but think that it conjured up a memory of his own trouble when he was young.

At the edge of Antioch and Pittsburg, against the western hills, Rose Hill Cemetery is halfway between the town sites of Somersville and Nortonville. In this small plot, the coal miner's graves had gone unprotected for many decades. The towns themselves have not stood on the sites since the coal industry dwindled and shifted, but the cemetery on the hill is unmistakable with its stand of exotic trees, headstones and monuments inside the wire fence enclosure.

Over the many years, Welsh families buried at Rose Hill have hosted hundreds of drunken teenage parties; beer bottles have been broken against their stones. I've heard of stolen markers being recovered in the 1970s, 1980s and 1990s. The park is called Black Diamond Mines, gated and guarded now, protected within the bosom of the East Bay Regional Parks District.

Another deep family secret that I am not supposed to know involves a grave robbery, an exhumation from a grave in Rose Hill Cemetery. My father was caught that night as one of the culprits. The incident occurred some time in the 1950s when he was a young man. My Uncle Dan was blamed for it, even though he was out of town with a strong alibi. It didn't make sense that Paul Lipton would do such a thing, but Dan Lipton, well that was another story.

In those days in the 1950s, and even into the 1970s, the Nortonville mines and the cemetery had two access roads. One road came in from

Somersville Road in Antioch and the other branched off of Kirker Pass, the steep road that cut between the cities of Concord and Pittsburg.

At that time, a person could drive a car all the way up to the cemetery gate. The paved roads made way for gravel and dirt. Now, a brutal hike is the only way to get from the parking lot to the cemetery. The first day I made the hike, I was out of breath and sweaty, trudging into a headwind.

I stepped around the coal slag and cow dung that littered the path. The cattle hoof prints were fat puddles full of the recent rain. I thought of e.e. cummings, "in just Spring, when the world is mud-luscious and puddle-wonderful."

As I walked by, the cows stared at me with bland interest and continued to chew their cud. One black cow stopped chewing long enough to register an expression of disgust and then let out a long moo. I mooed back.

My heart was pounding hard by the time I reached the cemetery. I came to atone for the sins of my father and for the sins of my son. I took a rest on a tree branch inside the cemetery gate. My car looked like a small toy in the parking lot below. I sat on the bough of the tree with the wind in my face. The gusts moved the tree bough like a cradle. The branch was strong enough to support me with my legs dangling. The willow strands wept over my head.

I began reading the headstones. The first one said:

Ruth

Wife of Jacob French

Died Sept.11, 1874

Aged 81 years

Ruth French was born in 1793 and her bones were safe in the ground, under my feet. Then I read another gravestone next to Ruth French:

Walter S. Jewett	Milton Jewett
Died	Died
April 21, 1869	August 20, 1874
Aged 19 years	Aged 16 years

I have paid many visits to Ruth French and the Jewett boys as a proxy for all the people from Nortonville, Somersville, Stewartville and environs, whose graves have ever been defiled by teenage vandals.

And each time I have driven out of Black Diamond Regional Park, I feel the road cut down, down, and the hills rise up, up around me. I feel a falling sensation as my car plummets into the canyon, the road winding down into the ravine, the barbwire fence plunging perpendicular to the dry creek bed.

The access road flattens near the ranger station. On one bright day, a humongous tarantula crossed up ahead. When I was close enough, I could make out its black hairy body and eight hairy legs treading across the road.

I have gone back to pay my respects on many occasions. Each day I walked the path, I spotted small white glazed ceramic fragments on the way to the cemetery. I gathered the shards of broken china dishes and put them in my pocket.

I have a special box at home that my father made for me out of blood wood, where I keep the chunks of bone china left on the trail near the old mining town sites. The porcelain-white misshapen chunks are small relics that connect me to the lives of the Somersville people. I imagine shattered teacups and saucers from long lost tea parties, now only mismatched shards that can never be reassembled.

I know very little about the incident with my dad in Rose Hill Cemetery. In my father's adolescent world, great shame and secrecy surrounded this event. Morrie was a prominent doctor and mayor of Antioch, and Mil was shaken by the behavior of the golden son. I also felt shaken when my golden son, Jack was expelled from high school for a stupid joke.

One day when I dragged myself through the gate to Rose Hill cemetery, heaving from the hike up the hill, I found a white fragment laying on Ruth French's grave. I was used to picking up china fragments and shards, but this small chip was natural and porous, like a tiny piece of bone. The bone from Ruth French's grave could be a chicken bone or a coyote or skunk bone, but to me it is a singular relic and a sign that my job is to keep the bone safe, to atone for the sins of my father and the sins of my son.

I felt the same sense of atonement during the trial and deliberations for the young man accused of murder. Our children are recipients of daily redemption and acquittal. It is in our fiber to protect them and forgive. The well of maternal forgiveness taps into the deepest aquifers of the collective unconscious. It is our goddess nature.

CHAPTER 19

SOCIALIST ROSE

Rose looks at me from the picture propped on my desk. She has worked with me, her face blooming with pride and encouragement. I would love to get to know her. I wish someone had saved her papers, her letters, her personal things, so I could gather baskets and armloads of the quintessential Rose Lipton, the woman I long to know.

The others I can apprehend, they are in my memory and my reach through keepsakes and heirlooms. I have baskets and armloads of Morrie and Mil. Rose eludes me.

When Rose Lipton died in 1961, my mom, Theresa Lipton, boxed up some of the books that had belonged to Rose.

"She had books that were Left, I mean really radical Left."

I wish I had her books. I'm trying to learn what Socialism is, but I still don't know. The phrase that resonates is "from each according to his ability, to each according to his need." I think if I understood Socialism, I'd understand my great grandmother better.

Rose Lipton lived for many years in Los Angeles and kept in touch with her nephew, Irving Goleman. Rose was a frequent visitor in the Goleman home in Stockton. In early 1949, Rose responded to a letter she had received from Irving and expressed her passion for Socialism and her upset at what he had written:

From Rose Lipton to Professor Irving Goleman

Saturday, February 19, 1949

3008a Chesapeake Ave

Los Angeles 16, Calif.

Dear Irv:

I have been wanting to answer your letter many times but never could decide what to say, and for that matter still don't know. However, since I will have to do it sometime, it might just as well be now… I was happy to know that you and your family are all well and that the development of your children is a source of great pleasure to you, I surely wish you more of the same in the future.

But now I am really coming to the part of your letter to answer and you will have to bear with me, if I don't make myself very clear. As to Professor Salo Baron's lecture on "Liberalism and the Jews," his explanation on living in "Liberalism without Liberty" or "Liberty without Liberalism" seems to me just juggling of words. For both of them go together, whether you put one or the other first.

As to Russia, neither you nor I, know how their system works, as we have not been there since their form of government changed from Zarist Feudalism to Socialism.

What we know is only what the corrupt press and radio feeds us and what they want us to know, unless you hear people, like Roggee Kenny and others who were there, not to forget the Dean of Canterbury Hewlitt Johnson, are allowed to tell us.

I do not have to go to Texas, which is in our U.S.A. to know, that Liberty and Equality do not go exactly hand in hand, we have fine examples right here in Calif.

Though I am very happy that you choose to pour out your thoughts to me as your second mother, I cannot help but feel that there was the thought of wanting to hurt my feelings in back of your mind, by pouring out your expression of hate for communism, a feeling I did not think you capable of. "Liberty and Equality" should not only sleep together but work together for Brotherhood for all Mankind, regardless of creed, color, or religion.

I also must disagree with you that "Judaism" is the solution, and it is not "Judaism" in the real sense of the word if you take in all the other isms, it is only "Socialism" which will accomplish to bring "real Brotherhood" to all "Mankind."

You also cannot be a "Jew" only, even amongst ourselves there are many (in fact too many factions) which make for disunity, like all other peoples, we are not only "Jews" but we are nationalistic, religious, political, and lots of other things.

However, I am happy, that the plight of our brethren brought you back to be a Jew again, which I am too and always was with all my heart and soul. I am feeling alright, am enjoying my little home and hope that you and Fay will come to visit me.

… Mor and Al and their families are fine, they all had the virus, which is quite prevalent right now. Hope to hear from you soon.

Love to you all,

Aunt Rose

Dare to know. What was happening when Rose wrote this letter to Irving Goleman? Events of the time: The McCarthy Era; Israeli statehood; strong political feelings against Commies; strong religious and political Zionist and anti-Zionist fervor.

I need a teacher or a mentor to pull me along, to guide me through.

At the very end of 1949, almost the last day of the year, Rose responded to a letter from Fay:

FROM ROSE LIPTON TO FAY AND IRVING GOLEMAN

December 27, 1949

Los Angeles, 16, Calif

Dear Folks,

It looks very much like we are not such good correspondents, but every once in a while there are occasions where we think of each other, for instance your rummaging around in some old papers or the New Year we get together. So here goes: "A Happy Healthy and prosperous New Year" to you all. When I came back from Dallas, where I was for 6 weeks, I found your letter among all other letters and magazines and was really very pleasantly surprised to see it. You see my correspondence with Irving had ended on quite a harsh note, and since he did not answer me I was sure he would not write again to me. He still did not, but your letter was just as welcome, and the snapshots of your two lovely daughters [Deborah and Judith] was a happy sight. Of course Danny is a very good looking boy even though he favors his dad. I can't say the pictures of my grandsons are beautiful, even though I know they are good looking, Morrie told me that they took a group shot and I am waiting to get it. You people keep busy with your family, with your social work and schoolwork; I was glad to hear that Irv did get that nice trip to Denver, I was there once upon a time for 10 days and I liked what I saw of it very much.

I never hear from June [Irving's sister] and am surprised that she does not write to you, she is probably in touch with her cousin Gloria [Bertha's daughter], but I never see her or her brother or cousins who live here, after all they are all young and I am old and we surely have different interests in life...

I can justly be proud of all my grandchildren and grand nieces and nephews as they are all good looking and smart. One thing puzzles me; according to all grandmothers and parents, all the kids are just that especially smart, but where are all the fools coming from?

...Again, wishing you all the best and a better year for all humanity as

ever.

Your loving Aunt Rose

What do I know of Irving? He was a brilliant professor, a classroom legend, the archetypal mentor. And those we call mentors have a tremendous capacity to build us up and to devastate us. I think children build towers and knock them down to echo and re-echo the alternating life pattern of soaring and crashing, meteoric rise and cataclysmic ruin. In my life, I built towering tall trees out of various scholars, professors, teachers and mentors. But this really wasn't fair, for they were also human, and in the end, the sign still reads, "Falling Trees."

When Ron Isetti retired from his post as U.S. and Asian history professor at Saint Mary's College, the customary review of his influences and accomplishments was printed:

...[Isetti's] mentor was Irving Goleman, a Stockton City College world literature professor. Goleman began each class by writing a quote from Roman poet Terence on the board: "I am human, therefore nothing human can ever be alien to me." The sentiment resonated with Isetti, encouraging him to view history as an opportunity to study different cultures. In this spirit, he added Asian history to his graduate studies at Berkeley in the early 1970s.

In his notes to Wilderness, the famous Jazz artist, Dave Brubeck, wrote:

I am not affiliated with any church. Three Jewish teachers have been a great influence on my life —Irving Goleman, Darius Milhaud, and Jesus. I am a product of Judaic-Christian thinking. Without the complications of theological doctrine, I wanted to understand what I had inherited in this world —both problems and answers —from that cultural heritage.

A man named John Whiting, one of Irving Goleman's former students wrote the following in 1998:

Half a century ago my college education began with a remarkable man named Irving Goleman. Professor Goleman was a sad, hollow-eyed Jew who carried the world on his stooped shoulders. He had been to the edge of the abyss and stared down into it. What he saw was so horrifying, but at the same time so avoidable, that he was driven to impart his vision to his students — even from the occasional depths of depression, in which he had been known to lie on his back atop his desk, delivering his lecture from this funereal position. He seemed to care for nothing except knowledge and the sharing of it — there was never time enough to impart it all. He organized all of human creativity along great temporal arcs on the blackboard, in which civilizations began in primitive simplicity, ascended towards classical rationality, and then declined into romantic decadence. Everything seemed to fit into these schemes, whether they were applied to ancient Greece, western Europe, or the cultural history of China or India... they provided an assurance of order, a guarantee that we were living in a rational if indifferent universe.

Apparently this was not enough; years later I would be told that my beloved mentor had committed suicide.

This hit me like the dull thud of a bell that is immobilized and cannot ring. It was never spoken out loud. I called my dad immediately.

"I have a question."

"Okay, I'd be happy to help you if I can."

"How did Irving Goleman die?"

I sensed discomfort in the pause on the other end of the line.

"Well, he was ill, but I was told by my father that Irving had spoken about suicide. But I don't really know. That is just what my father said to me. I don't know the real story."

"I'll ask Judy."

"But that might upset or offend her."

"Maybe Dan knows."

"I don't know. Maybe he does."

"What year was that?"

"Hmmm, lemme see. Well, Irving was still alive when I started college, before I went away to Carnegie Tech, around 1957 or 1958. The Goleman's offered to let me stay at their place in Stockton, because it would be more conducive to academic success." My dad chuckled at the irony, "That wasn't what I was interested in at the time."

I left it at that and changed to a new topic, but the dull thud resounded in my belly. And in my bones I felt a powerful resolve - *Sapere Aude* - Dare to Know.

I reeled back to that day in Stockton, when I had driven Naomi from the airport, and I remembered that the few small things that were said about Irving by his widow, Fay, and his daughters were in a faraway tone like a muffled bell -- not spoken. I was interlaced with the Goleman family on that day in Stockton, but Irving was the only strand that connected me to the Golemans, the unspoken, broken strand. Later I asked my Uncle David the same question.

"I already asked my dad this, but he doesn't really know."

"Well, your father can't remember shit."

"Do you know how Irving Goleman died?"

David gave a big sigh before he answered. "Well, there's an official story and there's a rumor. The story is that he got cancer. The rumor is that he committed suicide. But nobody ever talks about it. Nothing has ever been said."

I kept asking the question about Irving's death, but the documents and tributes said too little for me to know what to believe.

I asked my Uncle Dan, "Do you know how Irving Goleman died?"

"Pancreatic cancer."

"Does Judith talk much about her dad?"

"She keeps asking me what I remember of her father."

"What do you say?"

"I remember him as a kindly man who smelled of pipe tobacco."

The same way Rose unearthed herself by leaving me the locket, and my grandmother Mil's writings found their way into my hands, I heard the call of Irving Goleman's spirit wanting to be spoken. He is lost in the damaged memory. I don't know if Irving succumbed to pancreatic cancer or committed suicide. Morrie knew.

I can't imagine carrying the weight of what my grandfather knew. Morrie knew that Deborah Goleman was pregnant before she married Leonard, and he kept it quiet.

Morrie must have known my mother had given birth before. He was her doctor, her OB-GYN and took care of my mom when she was pregnant with my brother. Morrie must have known, but he never questioned why my mom already had episiotomy scars. She must have had episiotomy scars, no babies were born in the 1950s and early 1960s without knocking out the laboring mother and performing an episiotomy. If he didn't know, it was because he didn't want to know.

When I was born in 1963, I was delivered by my Grandpa Morrie Lipton. The newspaper clipping from the Antioch Ledger announced that my birth really made news, that I was the first girl born on the Lipton side of the family in 56 years, but that was a lie.

We found out the family secret so many years later. In March of 1960, my secret long-lost sister Debbie had been born in Pennsylvania. Debbie was the first grandchild, the first great grandchild to Rose, and the long-wished for girl in the family. Debbie was the first girl born in 53 years. My grandfather's baby sister, Jenny, had been the last female Lipton born. Jenny had died as a child so long ago.

In July of 1961, my great grandmother Rose died. She never knew her great-granddaughter, Debbie. Rose never saw any of the great-grandchildren. My brother Tom was born on Rose's birthday, November 1, four months after she died.

In January, 1962, six months after Rose Lipton's death, Irving Goleman died. And my grandfather knew something about Irving's death. He knew more than he would say.

Morrie knew the truth about Deborah Goleman's pregnancy. He kept her confidence when she was a young woman. When Morrie attended my mother, he must have known about her first baby, at least in his bones he knew.

Morrie knew the secrets of his past and his own excesses. He had gambled too hard, smoked too much and worked late hours. As a doctor, Morrie diagnosed and healed his patients and listened to their secrets. He must have known his own lungs were declining from the wear and tear of laughing, breathing and working. His heart was tired from pumping blood through clogged arteries.

Morrie knew that the years he had spent with Mil were folding in, collapsing on themselves. When the necessity of child-rearing and fortune-making was past, Mil and Morrie had less and less in common. They had spats and cold wars of distant glares and long silences.

First Morrie lost his mother, Rose. Then he lost his cousin, mentor and friend, Irving Goleman. My grandmother Mil wrote this note on steno paper perforated on the top:

CYNTHIA LIPTON

*F*ROM MIL TO MORRIE

April 7, 1964

Antioch, Calif.

Dear Morrie,

I cannot leave without saying thank you. Thanks for the many wonderful years we did have together. Thanks for three wonderful sons. Thanks – oh, for everything that was good and precious and dear.

I'm sorry we cannot seem to get along, but __! Perhaps we can be friends, at least.

Yours – for better or worse,

Mil

Knowing so many secrets about the beginning of life and the end of life must have been a heavy weight on Morrie's heart. In 1968, Morrie was stricken by a heart attack, cardiac arrest, and died at age 63.

Irving was also 63 when he died, six years before.

CHAPTER 20

BARE ROOTED

———

I was thinking about the edges of things, the seams, where night is stitched to day at dawn and at dusk, the margins and the edges of towns along the tracks. Like Knapp's Kozy Korner on the road from Antioch back home to Pittsburg.

I headed down the embankment into the Eucalyptus grove in Crockett one evening. I heard the caws of the turkey vultures from high in the gum trees; the crepuscular creatures must have smelled something dead along the banks of the Carquinez Strait.

My dog herded me along the path and crashed through the branches as we headed down past the abandoned structure I call the Moonshiner's Shack. Farther ahead, past a turn in the path, I saw a hollow tree. Out of curiosity, I reached my hand in the hole and found somebody's glass crack-pipe hidden in the hollow. The pipe was plugged with mud. I turned it over in my hand and put it back in its hiding place.

I shook my head at the sadness of this person's secret. Secrets can be as dangerous as drugs. Why do humans seek drugs? Drugs put people on the edge, on the margin of normal life. Drug users find themselves on the street, in the woods, smoking meth until their teeth fall out. Meth families end up staying with friends and relatives as long as the welcome holds. Their kids talk about all their stuff that is in a storage locker next to the freeway in Concord. Basement uncles keep adding to the junk that has accumulated in front of the houses.

Like Irving Goleman, I believe there is genius in every human being. Professors and homeless addicts all have the same human story. "I am human; therefore nothing human can ever be alien to me."

The dog nudged me out of my thoughts and put me back on the path, circling my legs, herding me toward home. As I trudged home, I thought about how secrets unravel. I thought about how my sister, Debbie, must have felt, knowing she was genetically Italian, living as a Jewish girl, wondering about and finally coming to know her birth parents.

I thought about how my great-grandmother, Rose, must have felt, leaving her home country, losing her daughter, making a life in Chicago and Los Angeles.

I thought about how my mother, Theresa, must have felt, passing that bundle over to the lawyer in the back seat of the cab in Pittsburgh, Pennsylvania.

Before I knew it I was home.

My house in Crockett is as old as the Society of American Folklore, built somewhere around 1890. When we moved in I found the walls stuffed with ancient crumbling 1887 newspapers. The historical insulation disintegrated like ash on touch.

The old house has been changed over the years. When we dismantled the entryway downstairs, we found old Coca Cola metal signs used as roofing material, a sign of recycling and thrift during the early 1900s.

The thrift of World War I was all over the slick colored pages of the 1917 and 1918 Saturday Evening Posts nailed up as insulation in my pantry. What things I find in the walls of my house are my archaeological inheritance, communications from the past.

Later, I met my Mormon stepdaughter. It was a matter of time; the news was not completely unexpected, because Kennan once told me that he may have fathered a girl before we met. Deanna was raised by her grandparents.

I thought about how my stepdaughter, Deanna, must have felt, learning when she was 10 or 11 years old, that she was adopted, that the woman she thought was her oldest sister was really her mother, that her father was a man named Kennan.

Deanna was raised by her grandparents as a conservative Mormon and studied at the satellite campus of Brigham Young University in Idaho. When we met her, I was startled to see how unquestionable the familial resemblance was. There was no question about her paternity. Her hands were Kennan's hands, from the shape of the fingers and the fleshy digits, the knuckles down to the bitten off nails. We talked about DNA paternity testing, but it was pointless. "Well, is there any doubt she's his? She looks just like a Shaw."

Mother Teresa of Calcutta said that "loneliness and the feeling of being unwanted is the most terrible poverty."

For this reason, the Mormons work at redemption. According to the words of Boyd K. Packer, from *Redemption of the Dead*, Ensign, Nov 1975, 97:

"Here and now then, we move to accomplish the work to which we are assigned. We are busily engaged in that kind of baptism. We gather the records of our kindred dead, indeed, the records of the whole human family; and in sacred temples and baptismal fonts, designed as those were anciently, we perform these sacred ordinances."

In digging up my roots, I have gotten embedded with the fathers, the mothers and the children in order to understand my place in the human experience. In America, we have all been scattered. Long gone is any experience of the European, long-standing, traditional, homogeneous, well-established, perennial sense of culture and homeland. We are a wild and scattered people.

I'm a direct product of the immigrant history of my own blood ancestors. Then I married into a different family line. No wonder we long for our kindred dead. My sister must have felt, like my stepdaughter must have felt -- bare-rooted, detached from parents.

Bare-rooted is the feeling of orphans and people who learn they were adopted and their birth parents are unknown -- the feeling of Diaspora, the scattered. Mormons, Jews, Dustbowl Okies and Voortrekkers share this root bare feeling.

I started distilling the family history, through ship passenger manifests, census records, pictures and letters. I have begun to fit my predecessors into a framework of this century, this hundred-something-year span between circa 1900 and circa 2010, where I am writing this book.

My grandparents, Morrie and Mil couldn't remember a time before powered flight was possible. My parents, Paul and Theresa don't remember the days before penicillin, a time when people used to die regularly of sepsis and infection.

My husband Kennan and I can't fathom a world without television. TV has always been there for cartoons on Saturday morning and *Mutual of Omaha's Wild Kingdom* at night. My kids, Jack and Carolyn, are oblivious to a world without the Internet. The telecommunications satellites are as reliable to them as the moon, the sun and the stars.

In 1907, Rose and baby Morrie got off the Kaiser Wilhelm der Grosse at Ellis Island. In 2007, one hundred years later, I went to visit Rose and Morrie and Mil on the night of the full moon. I sneaked in the broken back fence of the cemetery and burned candles on their three names with a sprinkling of coarse ground bloodroot to honor the family.

I dug my ancestor's grave dirt and paid for it with silver dimes and whiskey. I carried the dirt back with me to my home in Crockett to keep as a relic, to connect me to my forebears. As long as I have their DNA in my cells and their dirt in a jar, they are still with me.

I can read their thoughts and minds from the grave. Their essential human experience extracted before senescence, wilting, aging. They live forever because they have written down their words.

There would never be enough Rose. It takes sixty roses to distill one drop of Rose Otto. I'd never have enough botanical matter to distill even a single drop. Distillation wasn't the only way. I researched other methods, like enfleurage. In enfleurage, pure fat and rose petals are pressed between glass plates in a frame. After a few days in their fatty bed, the depleted petals are removed and replaced with a fresh harvest. Over time, with repeated cycles, the fat becomes saturated with the smell, the absolute essence, Rose Absolute.

King James Version, Psalm 65:11-12 shouts and sings to me:

Thou crownest the year with thy goodness; and thy paths drop fatness. They drop upon the pastures of the wilderness: and the little hills rejoice on every side.

The images of Google Earth and Google Maps and Google Street View are bounced off telecommunications satellites that track the global positions of cities and memories. I find the coordinates of my life and history, and plot the longitude and latitude of the points that mark who I am, down to the degrees and minutes of my story.

I have tried to know Rose through a few scant mentions and memories. Letters are scarce, but I do know her handwriting. If only I had Rose's things. Stories and memories are evoked by the objects and things that have touched me in my own life –- my childhood, objects touched by my parents and grandparents, the baby clothes my children wore.

In the regression of the infinity mirrors, Rose's generation recedes from view. So few things remain that belonged to Rose; Rose's locket, her opera glasses and the tattered leather case tell me Rose was cultured, sentimental, affluent and educated.

I believe Rose is pleased with the progress made by her offspring. Her daughter and sons have died, her grandkids have grown old, her great grandkids are in mid-life, and the great, great grandbabies are coming of age.

I have preserved Rose, pressed in the pages of a heavy book, a single bloom, between tissue paper. The smell is long gone and the color has faded under the weight of the *Oxford English Dictionary*, Volumes 1-20. I am her namesake and she is my keepsake.

Rose is preserved in pages and pages of words -- our language, our stories and memories on paper -- life beyond death.

LIPSTEIN/LIPTON SELECT FAMILY TREE

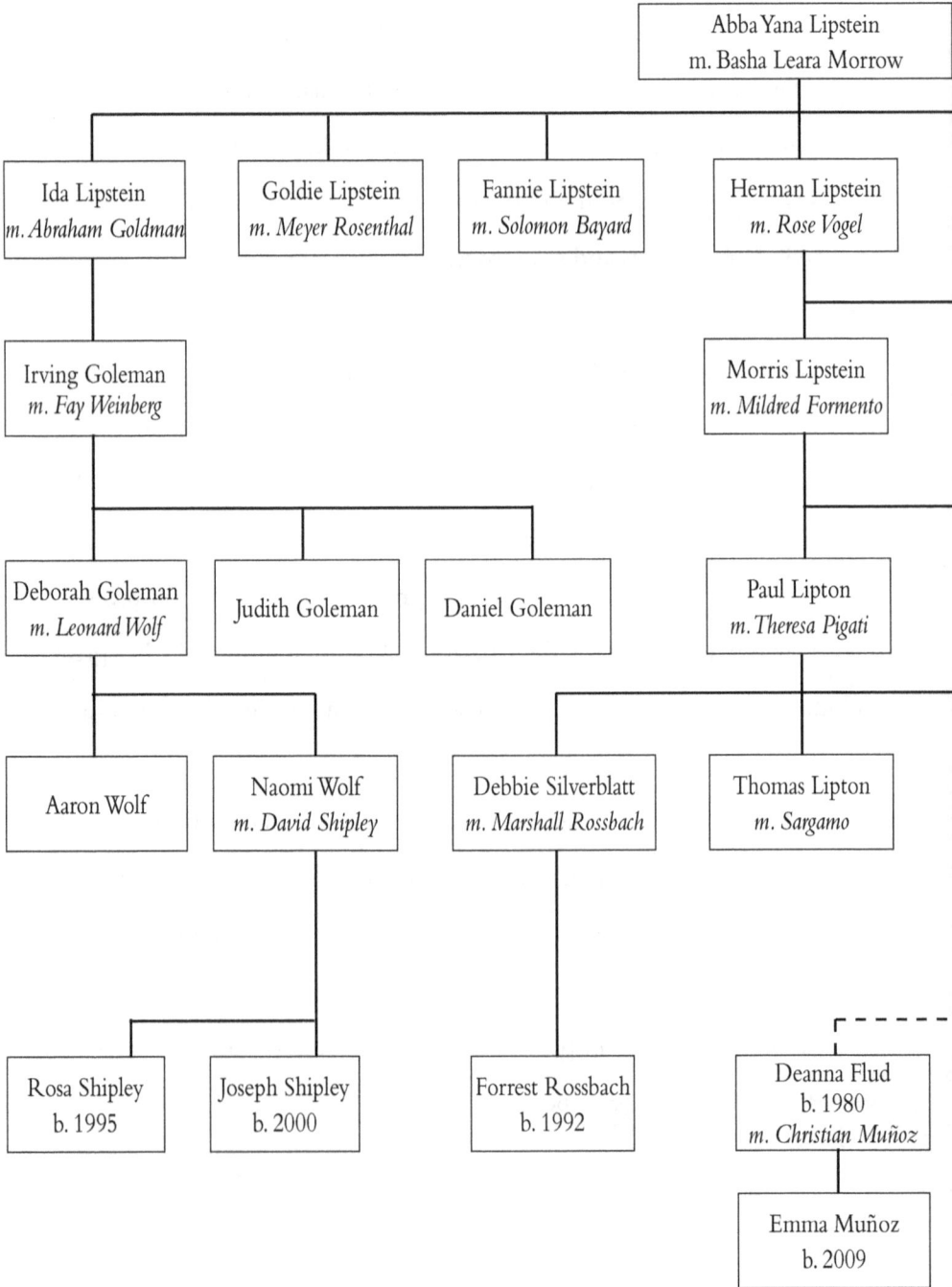

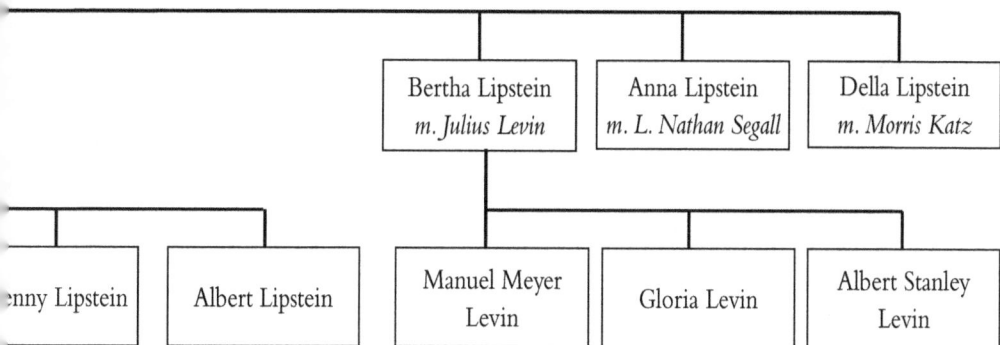

Bertha Lipstein *m. Julius Levin*	Anna Lipstein *m. L. Nathan Segall*	Della Lipstein *m. Morris Katz*	

:nny Lipstein	Albert Lipstein	Manuel Meyer Levin	Gloria Levin	Albert Stanley Levin

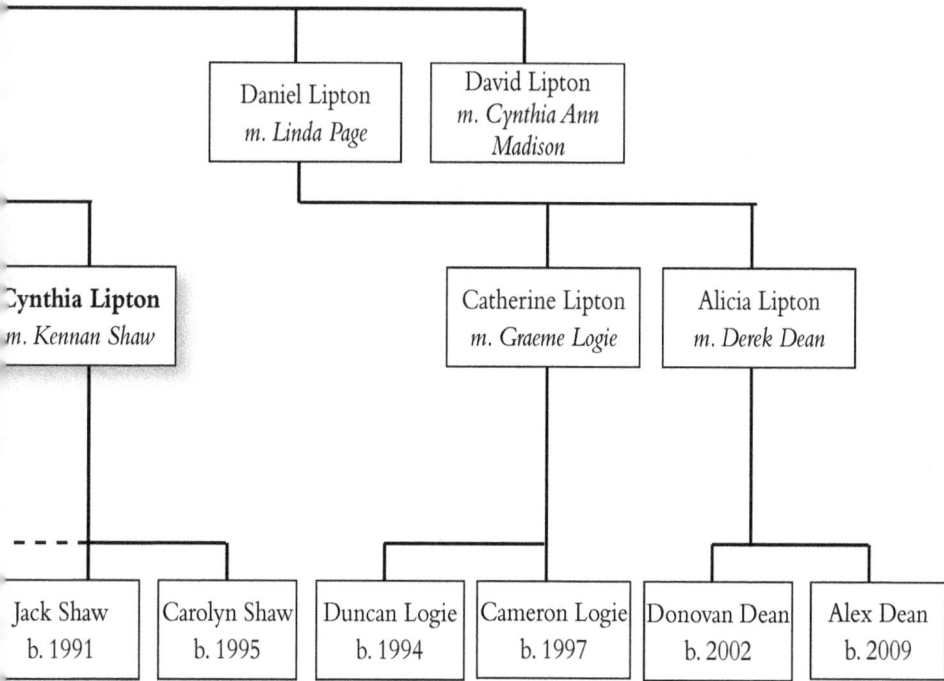

Daniel Lipton *m. Linda Page*	David Lipton *m. Cynthia Ann Madison*

:ynthia Lipton *m. Kennan Shaw*	Catherine Lipton *m. Graeme Logie*	Alicia Lipton *m. Derek Dean*

Jack Shaw b. 1991	Carolyn Shaw b. 1995	Duncan Logie b. 1994	Cameron Logie b. 1997	Donovan Dean b. 2002	Alex Dean b. 2009

ABOUT THE AUTHOR

Cynthia Lipton was born in Antioch, California. She lives with her

husband and their two children in Crockett, California.

Distilling Rose is her first book.

www.ingramcontent.com/pod-product-compliance
Lightning Source LLC
LaVergne TN
LVHW011219080426
835509LV00005B/208